OXFORD INTENSIVE ENGLISH COURSES

FAST FORWARD 2

CLASSBOOK

VAL BLACK
MAGGY McNORTON
ANGI MALDEREZ
SUE PARKER

OXFORD UNIVERSITY PRESS

Oxford University Press, Walton Street, Oxford OX2 6DP

Oxford
New York Toronto Melbourne Auckland
Petaling Jaya Singapore Hong Kong Tokyo
Delhi Bombay Madras Calcutta Karachi
Nairobi Dar es Salaam Cape Town

and associated companies in
Berlin Ibadan

OXFORD ENGLISH and the OXFORD ENGLISH LOGO
are trademarks of Oxford University Press

ISBN 0 19 432304 8

First published 1987
Third impression 1989

Set in Helvetica light by S & S Press
Printed in Hong Kong

The authors and publishers would like to thank all the copyright holders for their permission to reproduce the extracts in this book.

The table from *Social Trends 1982* (p. 4), the extracts from the Office of Fair Trading's leaflet (p. 16) and the *Neighbourhood Watch* leaflet (p. 49) are reproduced with the permission of the Controller of Her Majesty's Stationery Office. The *Market Gardener* and *Lorry Driver* texts (pp. 5–6) by permission of the Sunday Telegraph Magazine. The consumer letters (p. 16) extracted by kind permission of Family Circle. The extracts from the *Jobclub* leaflet (p. 22) by permission of the Manpower Services Commission. *The Dog Exercising Machine* (p. 35) is from an idea by Edward De Bono. The extract from *Things Fall Apart* by Chinua Achebe (p. 38) is reproduced by kind permission of Heineman Educational Books Ltd. ©. The extract from the *Citizens Advice Bureau* leaflet (p. 46) by permission of the National Association of Citizens Advice Bureaux. *Sandy Takes The Bridal Path To Misery* (p. 81) from the Daily Mail by permission of Mail Newspapers plc. *Festival Of Chinese Culture* (p. 87) by permission of the Cardiff Post. The article on the Notting Hill Carnival (p. 87) by permission of City Limits. The article (p. 88) by permission of the Edgware and Kingsbury Recorder. The article (p. 89) by permission of the South Wales Echo and the Cardiff Post.

The publishers have been unable to trace and would be pleased to hear from the copyright holders of the recording (p. 39) adapted from African Myths And Tales. *The original extracts from* The First Men *(pp. 74–75). The recording (p. 85) of Revd Martin Luther King Jr., believed to be the copyright of the Joan Daves Agency, 515 Madison Avenue, New York, N.Y., 10022. The publishers would also be pleased to hear from any other parties who feel they hold rights to any of the texts included.*

The publishers would also like to thank the following for their permission to reproduce photographs and logos:

Barbican Centre; Britain on View; The British Horse Society; The Camping and Caravanning Club; J. Allan Cash; Central Office of Information; Bruce Coleman; Donald Cooper; The Daily Telegraph; The Dance Library; DAS; Debenhams; The Financial Times; Format Photographers; Richard and Sally Greenhill; The John Hillelson Agency; The Hutchinson Library; Illustrated London News Picture Library; The Kobal Collection; The Mansell Collection; The National Trust; Network Photographers; Ramblers' Association; Royal Society for the Prevention of Accidents; Royal Society for the Protection of Birds; South Riverside Community Development Centre, Cardiff; Spectrum Colour Library; Times Newspapers Ltd; Western Mail and Echo; Youth Hostel Association.

and the following for their time and assistance:

Cambridge and County Folk Museum; The Feathers Hotel, Woodstock; Mataam Marakesh Restaurant, Torquay; Michel's Brasserie, Oxford; Moody Menswear, Oxford; Noremarsh Junior School, Wootton Bassett; Pickfords Travel, Oxford.

Illustrations by:

Peter Dennis; Julie Douglas, Carolyn Gowdy; Karen Ludlow; James Ody; Ian Penning; Bill Piggins; Joanna Quinn; Mark Rowney; Nick Sharratt; Anthony Sidwell.

Photography by:

Christopher Hurst; Rob Judges; Mark Mason; Alison Souster; Eric Tall.

To the student

This book tries to help you practise and learn more English in a meaningful and realistic way. In order to do this the Classbook emphasizes spoken interactive skills. We hope that the variety of topics and exercises in the book will stimulate you to express yourself to the other members of your group and, most of all, that you will enjoy your learning.

The accompanying Resource Book and Resource Cassette provide additional material to help you practise reading and listening skills, together with work on grammatical structures which we feel are important for you at this stage. (Did you understand that relative clause? See Resource Book Review Unit 2!) There is also guidance on how to get the most from your dictionary, a few tips on spelling, and work to extend your vocabulary. Answers are given at the back of the book so that you can work at your own speed during or after the course.

So . . . work hard and have fun!

Acknowledgements

Many people came up with advice, suggestions and, above all, a lot of support during the prolonged gestation that became *Fast Forward 2*. Particular thanks to Sue Mace who provided such a welcome geographical half-way house and soothed our shattered nerves with tea, sympathy and yoga!

We gained much welcome support and advice from our colleagues at various institutes; South Devon College of Arts and Technology, Torquay; College of St Mark and St John, Plymouth; Bell School, Cambridge; Bell Language Institute, London; Regent School, London; St Giles School, Brighton; Godmer House, Oxford. Very special thanks here to Jeremy Parrott, Brian Cox, Sue Burkhill, Malaysian Matriculation Students, Dave and Margaret Hutchinson, Jane Carne, Anna Allen, Tony Pearson, Pauline Taylor, Leon Winston, Jerome Betts, Andrew Dunn, Graeme Burn, Rod Bolitho, Tor Nicol, Dominique Vivez, Gilly Cunningham, Gill Hadfield, Amanda Kelman, June Hillyard, Anne Taylor, Andy Hopkins, Rietta Marshall, Joanna Strange, Tony Wright, Pam Murphy, David Killick, John McFarling, Alison Thomas, Bob Weaver and Judith Whittleton.

Children who came up with material should also be mentioned; Duncan and Kate Parker, Susanna Thain, Helen Camilleri, Gary and Jeff Malderez, Daniel and Hannah McNorton, Lara Dunn, and, of course, Josie.

Much of our material was based around conversations with friends, neighbours, very slight acquaintances, and the milkman! We would like to say thank you to Sgt. Blair, Mrs Hamilton and Mrs Prior, Mrs Black, Sean Ford, Viv Bolitho, George Inglis, Steve McDermott, John Curtin, Rod Ellis, John Dunnet, Mrs A. J. Cook, Tom Doig of the Cambridge County Folk Museum, Armin Kleger, and Acora.

Thanks, too, for the love and support from our long-suffering families and close friends.

We acknowledge also the influence and inspiration of ideas from John Morgan and Mario Rinvolucri, Anne Pechou, Gertrude Moskowitz, Rod Bolitho and Chris Candlin.

Finally, thanks for the much-needed encouragement that came from David Sawer, Yvonne de Henseler, Coralie Green, Sue Sharp, Sally Foord-Kelcey, Nicky Stratford, and indeed all the support staff at Oxford University Press who encountered 'the gang of four'.

Val Black Maggy McNorton Angi Malderez Sue Parker

SCOPE AND SEQUENCE CHART

Page	Unit	Communicative Functions	Topics and Vocabulary	Language Focus
2	Introductory Unit	Introductions	Getting to know each other Leisure Work	Present Simple Question forms Relative clauses: who Gerund/Infinitive
7	1	Asking for and giving directions Asking for information Saying where places are Describing places	Edinburgh Tourist information Towns	Prepositions
11	2	Offers and requests Arrangements Suggestions Hopes and plans	Food and drink Business conferences Entertainment	Modals: could/would/can Present Continuous for future arrangements Degrees of certainty
16	3	Complaining Apologizing Offering to put things right Accepting or refusing offers	Consumer problems Shopping	Present Perfect
20	**Review Unit 1** Part 1	Revision	Multicultural Britain Eating out in Britain Unemployment	Revision
	Part 2	Project	Finding out about other countries	
26	4	Describing things Describing people	Natural things Personality	Word order Relative clauses
31	5	Comparison Describing processes	Statistics Developing world Chewing gum	Passives Sequencing
36	6	Describing past actions and events	Customs and beliefs Myths	Past tenses Sequencing
40	**Review Unit 2** Part 1	Revision	Britain: people, places and accents	Revision
	Part 2	Simulation	Dalelakemoor	

INTRODUCTORY UNIT

Introductions

Getting to know each other Leisure Work

A BREAKING THE ICE

1 Ask the people in your class questions to complete this exercise.

Find a person who . . .

has got two sisters
likes dogs
speaks three languages
likes pop music
wants to go to Scotland
hates sport
rides a bicycle
enjoys singing
plays the piano
is interested in football
can dance
can climb

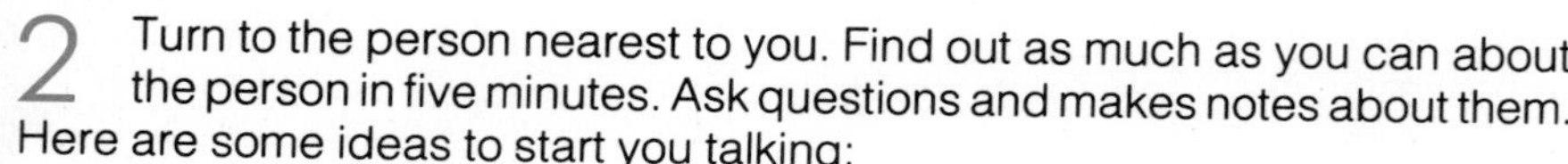

2 Turn to the person nearest to you. Find out as much as you can about the person in five minutes. Ask questions and makes notes about them. Here are some ideas to start you talking:

Now make groups of four. Introduce your partner to the other people in your group and tell them a little about him/her.

B INTRODUCTIONS

1 Look at these phrases:

This is . . .	Hi!
I'd like you to meet . . .	Hello!
I'd like to introduce you to . . .	I'm honoured to meet you.
I'd like to present . . .	Pleased to meet you.
Please allow me to present . . .	How do you do?

Which phrases are formal and which phrases are informal?

2 Use an appropriate phrase to introduce your partner to other people in the class.

3 How would you introduce these people to each other? What would they say?

A		B	
a close friend	to	your mother	in the street
a close friend		another friend	at a party
your new secretary		your boss	in the office
your lawyer		your bank manager	at the bank
a new client		a business colleague	at a business lunch
a V.I.P. speaker		the audience	at a meeting
your sister		a business colleague	in a pub

Work in groups of three. Two people play roles A or B and the third person must introduce them using appropriate language. Act out the different situations given.

4 Listen to the three short conversations. Try to decide:

1 where the people are
2 what relationship they have to each other

C TALKING ABOUT LEISURE

1 What do British people do in their spare time?

On the next page are the results of a survey of leisure activities made in 1981. Work with a partner to find out the following information:

1 Which are the two most popular activities away from the home?
2 Which are the two most popular home-based activities?
3 Which are the two most popular sports?
4 How many people go to the cinema?
5 How many people do gardening?
6 How many people read a daily newspaper?
7 How many people do the pools?
8 How many hours of TV do British people watch?
9 How many people play squash?
10 How many people enjoy doing home repairs (DIY)?

LEISURE SURVEY

*The figures show the percentage of British people who take part in the activities every month.**

Away from the home

cinema	10%
seaside	7%
country	4%
evening classes	1½%
theatre, opera, ballet	4½%
a meal	40%
a drink (pubs etc.)	54%
dancing	14%

Home-based

records and tapes	64%
gardening	45%
needlework or knitting	28%
DIY/house repairs	37%
books	57%

Sports

indoor swimming	6%
fishing	1%
football	3%
tennis	1%
keep-fit or yoga	1%
squash	2%
darts	7%
billiards, snooker, pool	7%
walking (2 miles or more)	18%
cycling	1%

Other

watching football	4%
football pools	19%
bingo	8%
daily newspaper	72%**
TV	20 hours p.w.

** Based on a four-week period. The sample size was 10478 men, 12116 women.*
*** Approximate percentage based on newspaper sales.*

Source: Social Trends, 1982, Government Statistics Office, HMSO.

2 Now find out about the leisure interests of the people in your class. Plan a questionnaire to find out:

1 which activities they like
2 how often they do these activities

Plan your questionnaire like this:

	yes	no	often	sometimes	rarely	every day	once a week	once a fortnight	(other answer)
1 Do you like going to the cinema? **2** Are you interested in opera? **3** . . . **4** . . . **5**									

Does anyone share your interests?

D

ASKING ABOUT JOBS

1 Work in pairs. On this page and the next are articles about two jobs. Read about one job each. Then interview each other to find out about the other job. Ask questions like this:

How much money . . . ?
How many hours . . . ?
How many weeks holiday . . . ?
What qualifications . . . ?
How . . . to work?
How long . . . the journey . . . ?
When . . . start work?
When . . . finish work?
What . . . like about your job?
What . . . dislike about your job?

Make a chart about the two different jobs, like this:

	Job A	**Job B**
Wages/Salary Hours Holiday Qualifications Travel to work Length of journey Start work Finish work Like Dislike		

Job A

Market gardener

Janet Anema, 44, is married with a teenage daughter and son. They live in Norfolk on the outskirts of Dereham within the grounds of her market garden, Hillside Nurseries, of which she is sole owner. She employs two full-time staff (plus casual staff of between six and 17) to tend six acres, three under glass. Main commercial crops are tomatoes, cucumbers, lettuces. Turnover is £90,000. Customers are mainly local retail shops; surplus produce goes to wholesale markets and to London. Janet Anema works in the nurseries; manages the staff; supervises the packaging of the vegetables; does the paperwork; liaises with customers and does some van deliveries.

EARNINGS Pays herself about £2,000 a year, sometimes slightly more or less depending on profits and the re-investment needed. PERKS Runs car and telephone off the business. Family eats the reject vegetables.

HOURS 5½-day week. 9 a.m. to 5 p.m. in the nursery; plus several hours' office work, two or three evenings a week. Holiday: "I try to get a fortnight a year".

CONDITIONS Very dirty work; wet and muddy. "On a hot day, you can be sweltering in 80–90°F in the greenhouses."

TRAINING Entirely self-taught. Left boarding school at 17 and started training at St Bartholomew's Hospital to become a nurse. Returned home after a few months. Was offered an old block of glasshouses on a nearby farm. Enjoyed "growing things" and, aged 19, obtained a £2,000 bank loan (with her father standing guarantor) to buy a small plot near her home.

PROSPECTS "Very bad at the moment. The Dutch government subsidizes its growers with cheap fuel to the extent that they can sell produce more cheaply than we can even produce." JOB SECURITY "Very slim: it was good at one time but in recent years we have only just broken even and last year we had to sell at a loss. This is crunch year for us. If we are not allowed to compete on equal terms we shall either have to sell up or convert to a different crop, like year-round lettuces, which would mean redundancies and a drastic reduction in my standard of living."

DRAWBACKS Getting very dirty and "I would earn far more working for someone else."

ATTRACTIONS Likes to be her own boss and "Nothing can be more satisfying than growing things, from a seed through to harvesting."

Job B

Lorry driver

John Underwood, 30, lives in Leamington Spa with his wife and two young children. He travels to work by scooter to Ellis Greaves Transport, which delivers freight all over England, Scotland and Wales. He drives a 32-ton Seddon articulated lorry. His responsibilites include: checking over the vehicle before starting, supervising the loading of freight and sometimes giving a hand, and planning the route.
EARNINGS £6,000 to £7,000 gross a year (depending on overtime). Basic pay is £78 for a 40-hour week. Overtime is paid at time-and-a-half (extra at weekends and a bonus of 2p for each loaded mile he drives). 50p "early start money" if he begins before 6.30 a.m. Overnight allowance: £9 (for digs and meals). PERKS Overalls. Occasional tips.
HOURS Variable. Overtime is an intrinsic part of the job and a 50–60 hour week is normal. Maximum allowed driving time is eight hours a day but loading/unloading can take hours. Holiday: four weeks.
CONDITIONS Alone for a lot of the time, and "you can get very bored". A lot of waiting around, particularly at docks. "Out in the open a lot; sheeting up a big load with the wind blowing can take hours." But there is a camaraderie with other drivers. He is a member of the TGWU.
TRAINING Left school at 15. Various jobs: factory, Royal Navy, shops. Then took a 14-day course at his own expense to obtain HGV Class 1 licence.
PROSPECTS "I don't really know."
JOB SECURITY Many transportation firms have been having a rough time in the present recession, and there have been a great many redundancies. But he says: "This firm is very good". Notice: one week.
DRAWBACKS Being away nights and "missing the wife and kids". Quite a tiring job at times.
ATTRACTIONS "You're your own gaffer out on the road."

2 Come to an agreement about the following questions:

Decide which job is . . .

1 the most dangerous?
2 the most exciting?
3 the most boring?
4 the most useful?
5 the most difficult?

3 Now describe *your* job (or the job you would like to do) to the people in your group.

LEARNING TO LEARN

Consider the following statements and then discuss your thoughts with other students.

I'm here because . . .

1 I want to really understand English grammar.
2 I want/need to get my English up to date.
3 I don't know enough words.
4 I've got an important English exam in two months' time.
5 I need better English for my job.
6 I want to speak *proper* English.
7 I can't understand English on the radio.
8 I need to write business letters.
9 I want to be able to read English better.
10 I wanted to have a holiday with a difference.
11 I just needed to get away.
12 I . . . . .

UNIT 1

A STRANGER IN TOWN

Asking for and giving directions Asking for information Saying where places are Describing places

Edinburgh Tourist information Towns

A FINDING YOUR WAY AROUND

1 Do you know the different ways of asking someone the way when you are in a strange town? Put some ideas in a table like this:

Excuse me,	can you tell me the way to George Street,	please?

And how can you say you don't know if someone asks *you* the way?

I'm awfully sorry,	I'm not really sure.	I'm a stranger here as well.

2 Work in pairs. Student A asks the way to the following places. Student B says he/she does not know the town. Use the language in A1.

hospital supermarket
station library
chemist post office

3 What about giving directions in a town that you *do* know? Imagine you live in Edinburgh. Study the map on the next page. A stranger stops you outside the College of Art (near Lauriston Place) and asks you the way:

How do I get from here to	John Knox House (3) Huntley House (5) the Assembly Rooms (10) the Scott Monument (6) the Palace of Holyroodhouse (11) the National Portrait Gallery (9)	please?

Take it in turns to ask for and give directions from the College of Art.

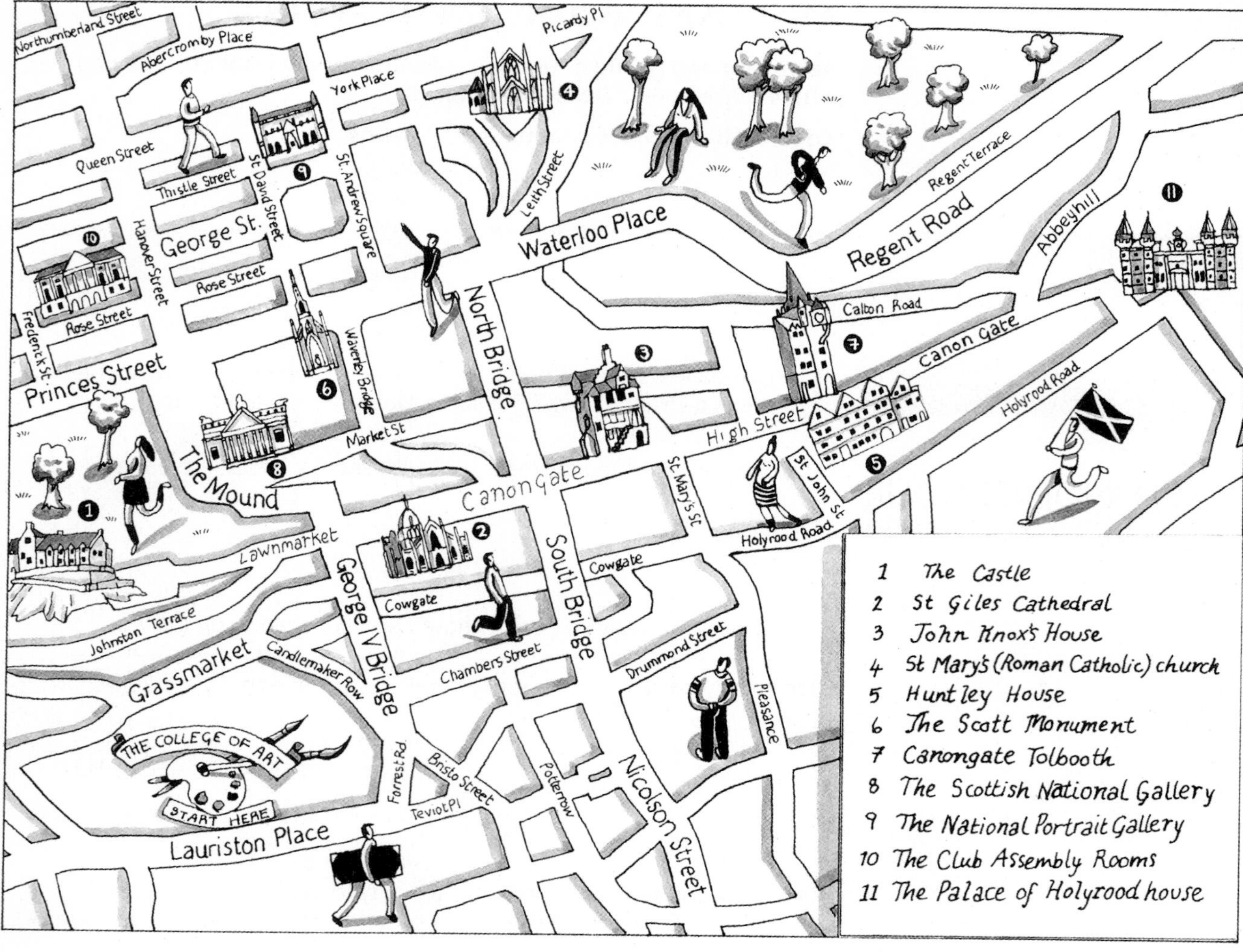

B

TOWN AND AROUND

1 In pairs (A and B) collect information about the town you are studying in. Limit yourselves to one theme or area of interest, e.g. museums, traditional crafts, bus tours, old houses, shops, etc. Read the information together and make sure you understand it.

2 Student A: you are the Information Officer. Stay where you are and make a sign to show the area of interest you have information about.

Student B: you are a Tourist. You want information about things to do in the next few days. Go round four Information Officers, collect the information and make a chart to refer to later.

	Area of interest	Name	Place	Times of opening	Price	Other
1						
2						

3 When the Tourists have all the information they need, swap roles with your Information Officer.

4 Compare your information with the rest of the class. Who has found the most interesting things to do?

C

TOWNS – REAL AND IMAGINARY

1 Draw a map of a town to include the following features and places:

a flyover
a T-junction
a pelican crossing
a roundabout
a railway
a bridge
a church
the Town Hall
a castle
the bus station
a museum
a university

Describe your map to a partner so that he/she can reproduce it.

2 Describe the town you come from to your group.

Is it a town or a village?
Is it in the north or the south of the country?
Has it got any old or unusual or interesting buildings?
Has it got a museum, art gallery, university, etc.?
What tourist facilities has it got?

3 In groups, plan your ideal town. Here are some ideas to start you thinking.

SPORT?

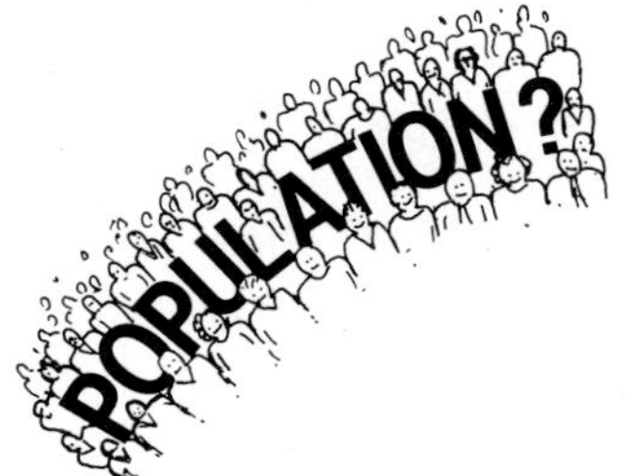

D

PLACES IN BRITAIN

1 Have you visited any other towns or places in Britain? Where were they? What were they like? Tell the other members of your group, and show them where they are on the map.

2 Now see if you can identify any of the missing names on the map.

E

LEARNING TO LEARN

Tick any of the statements below which seem to describe how you feel about learning a language. Then discuss your thoughts with others in your group.

1 It is extremely difficult to learn a language when you get older.
2 You forget a language if you don't use it.
3 People seem to take on a different personality when they speak another language.
4 Some people have a natural gift for learning languages.
5 It's possible to learn a language without a teacher.
6 Memorizing is an important part of learning.

UNIT

2

THE CONFERENCE

Offers and requests **Arrangements** **Suggestions** **Hopes and plans**
Food and drink **Business conferences** **Entertainment**

A THE FIRST EVENING

1 John Davis and Anne Wright are at a management conference. They have arrived at the hotel and are in the bar. Listen and decide the relationship (boss, employee, friend, business associate) between John, Anne, Robert and Sue.

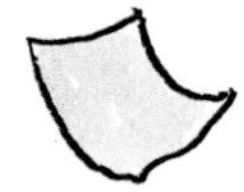

2 How would you . . .

1 offer a drink to your boss?
2 offer a drink to a friend?
3 offer dinner to your mother?
4 offer dinner to your father's colleague?
5 offer a drink to a colleague?

How might they accept or refuse your offer?

3 In groups of three, give yourselves roles, e.g. two friends and a boss, or three colleagues etc., and take turns to offer rounds of drinks.

B AT DINNER

1 The delegates are now at dinner. Listen. Who is a vegetarian?

Listen again and answer these questions.

1 How does Anne ask Robert to pass the menu?
2 How does John attract the waiter's attention?
3 How does Anne ask the waiter for a vegetarian dish?
4 How does Sue ask Anne to pass the water?
5 How does Sue ask John and Anne to wait for her?
6 Why does Sue want to go to her room?

2 How would you . . .

1 ask a friend to lend you a pencil?
2 ask a colleague to pass you the salt?
3 ask a friend to lend you a car?
4 ask your father to lend you some money?
5 ask your boss to explain something again?
6 ask your boss to get a new photocopier?

3 **Request game**

1 Make a list of five things to ask other people in the class to do. Remember, if it's a big thing you're asking you'll have to be more polite and more persuasive.
2 Move around the class making your requests. Try to get someone to agree to each request.

C THE CONFERENCE PROGRAMME

1 Look at the conference programme below. Imagine you are at the conference and choose which lectures you would like to attend. In pairs or small groups tell each other what you *are doing* tomorrow. You could begin like this:

A What *are you doing* first thing tomorrow?
B I think *I'm going* to 'Use and Abuse of Authority'. That should be interesting. What about you?
A I'm not sure what 'Elements of Management' includes, but *I'm going* to that. And then?
B Then *we're having* coffee!
A No, which lecture *are you listening* to next?
B . . . . .

1987 Management Conference Programme
Day 1

	Main Conference Hall	Vivien Suite	Raleigh Suite
9.15	Elements of Management	The Role of the Boss	Use and Abuse of Authority
10.30		**COFFEE**	
11.00	(a) Experiential Training	(a) Interview Techniques	(a) The Computerized Office – Hardware
12.30		**APERITIF**	
1.00		**BUFFET LUNCH**	
2.00	(b) Workshop	(b) Workshop	(b) Hands-on Workshop
3.30		**TEA**	
4.00	Transactional Analysis	Interpersonal Communication – Office Problems	(c) The Computerized Office – Software
5.00	Motivation Theories	Setting up In-Service Workshops	Pros & Cons of Pre-Planned Career Structures
6.30		**COCKTAILS**	
7.00		**DINNER**	

2 What arrangements have you got this week? What are you doing?

D SATURDAY EVENING

1 It's late Saturday afternoon, and the delegates are wondering what to do. Listen. Where do they decide to go?

2 Listen again, look at the advertisements, and answer these questions.

1. What doesn't Anne fancy doing?
2. What are the names of the three shows on at the local theatres?
3. Which is a musical? Which is a variety show? Which is a farce?
4. What doesn't Sue feel like doing?
5. When Anne phoned the restaurant, what do you think the person replied?

3 Listen again and fill in the gaps with the phrases that Anne and Sue use to make suggestions.

1. ________ ________ ________ a sauna?
2. ________ ________ ________ the receptionist?
3. I wonder ________ ________ ________ ________ what we could do in town this evening?
4. ________ ________ ________ ________ ________ along by the sea for a while.
5. OK. ________ go.
6. ________ ________ ________ ________ and find that Moroccan restaurant?

4 In small groups, decide what you're going to do either this evening or at the weekend.

E HOPES AND PLANS

1 Listen to Sue and Anne talking after a good meal in the Mataam Marrakesh. Has their friendship changed since the beginning of the conference?

2 Listen again and fill in the blanks.

Sue That was ______ . I love the way they cook lamb.
Anne Yes, superb. I love the fresh herbs in the salads too. And my vegetable curry was perfect.
Sue Mm, I feel good! Well, Anne, you've done well since I last saw you. ______ ______ ______ ______ ______ ______ now?
Anne Well, things are a little uncertain as the company ______ be taken over by a multinational.
Sue ______ ______ ?
Anne Well, ______ ______ ______ , ______ probably lose my job, but *I'm hoping* it won't come to that.
Sue You ______ ______ kept on.
Anne Yes, well, ______ ______ ______ fight anyway! What about you?
Sue Well, if I'm not promoted soon, ______ ______ ______ ______ jobs. I'm getting a bit bored! Oh, work's all right really. It's my cottage I'm excited about really. ______ ______ ______ redecorate first, and then ______ ______ ______ reorganize the garden. I can't wait!
Anne But ______ ______ ______ ______ jobs? You ______ have to move.
Sue Well, ______ ______ ______ this one at a huge ______ and buy a better one!
Anne Well, one thing is sure – ______ ______ ______ meet again on the conference circuit sooner or later.
Sue We could try writing this time. What's your address?

3 Look back at the dialogue and make a note of the phrases Anne and Sue use to express their hopes and plans. The first one was *I'm hoping* . . . Discuss which of the phrases seem to express more certainty about the future.

4 Your dreams have come true, and you are now famous. Imagine yourself as a celebrity, and think about where you live, what your life-style is like, what your plans for the future are. A reporter from an important international magazine is going to interview you.

In pairs, take it in turns to be the reporter and the celebrity.

F LEARNING TO LEARN

1 Agree or disagree with the following statements.

1 I'm rather shy about speaking in a group of people.
2 I don't like reading very much and I'm rather slow.
3 I like writing but I don't spell very well.
4 English people speak so fast and I don't see how I'm ever going to understand every word.

2 How do you learn new vocabulary? For example, do you . . .

1 learn 10 new words a day?
2 translate new words into your own language?
3 use a monolingual dictionary to understand new words?
4 record new words in a notebook? How? In alphabetical order? In groups of similar meaning? With drawings?

Compare your methods of learning new words with those of other students in the class.

UNIT 3

CONSUMER TIME

Complaining **Apologizing** **Offering to put things right** **Accepting or refusing offers**

Consumer problems **Shopping**

A CONSUMER PROBLEMS

1 Read these two letters from a consumer advice column. In one case the shop acted perfectly legally. Do you know which one and why?

Must I buy from this shop again?

I bought a pair of sandals, the end of a line, and the ankle strap broke the first time I wore them. The shoe shop wouldn't give my money back although they could not replace them. They said it was company policy to give a credit note which can be exchanged for other goods. I'm so angry – I don't want to buy more of their shoes. Must I accept their credit note?

Why can't I have my money back?

I bought a duvet cover with a pink design but when I got it home, I realized that the colour clashed with the rest of the bedroom. When I took it back, still in its wrapping, the shop would not return my money. Is the shop within its right to do this?

2 Have you ever had problems like these? What did you do? What could you do?

3 Read the following extract from the Office of Fair Trading's leaflet 'How to put things right', and decide how to reply to the letters in A1.

When you buy something you and the seller make a contract. Even if all you do is talk! The seller – not the manufacturer – must sort out your complaint.

The law has three rules:

1 Goods must be **of merchantable quality.** This means they must be reasonably fit for their normal purpose. Bear in mind the price and how the item was described. A new item must not be broken or damaged. It must work properly. But if it is very cheap, secondhand or a 'second' you cannot expect top quality.

2 Goods must be **as described** – on the package, a display sign or by the seller. Shirtsleeves should not be long if marked 'short' on the box. Plastic shoes should not be called leather.

3 Goods must be **fit for any particular purpose** made known to the seller. If the shop says a glue will mend china, then it should.

All goods—including those bought in sales—are covered (food too) if bought from a trader. For example, from shops, in street markets, through mail order catalogues or from door-to-door sellers.

B

COMPLAINING AND APOLOGIZING

1 Match the four recorded conversations with the photographs, and then make notes of the language used to complain, apologize, and accept or refuse offers.

Conversation . . . . .

Complaint . . . .
Apology . . . .
Offer . . . .
Acceptance . . . .

Conversation . . . . .

Complaint . . . .
Apology . . . .

Conversation . . . . .

Complaint . . . .
Apology . . . .
Refusal . . . .
Offer . . . .
Refusal . . . .

Conversation . . . . .

Complaint . . . .
Apology . . . .
Offer . . . .

2 In pairs, take turns to imagine yourself in these situations. Practise the language of complaints, apologies, offers, refusals and acceptances.

1 You bought an expensive jumper last month; now it's shrunk.
2 You ordered soup but they've brought you a prawn cocktail.
3 You asked for a double bed and you've got two singles.
4 You've just bought some cream. It smells funny.
5 The wine tastes awful!
6 The brochure said the hotel would arrange trips. It hasn't.
7 The shop assistant has just given you change for a £5 note. You gave her £10.
8 The cutlery at your table looks dirty.

C APOLOGIES

1 Frank Broughton, manager of F. G. Broughton's department store, has an apology to make to his assistant manager, Miss Bridges, for missing a meeting. She too has a confession to make. Listen.

1 Why did he miss the meeting?
2 Why does Miss Bridges apologize too?

2 How would you apologize in these situations? Work in pairs. One of you apologizes in each case, and offers to put things right. The other accepts the apology.

1 You broke three glasses at your friend's party last night.
2 You've lost a book you borrowed. Now it's time to tell your friend.
3 You've just burnt a hole in your landlady's carpet. She's in the garden.
4 You are half an hour late for the lesson.
5 You've just spilt coffee on your friend's sofa. She's in the kitchen.
6 You didn't do your homework last night.

3 Think back to an event in your life when something went wrong and you had to apologize or complain. What happened? What did you say? Exchange stories with a partner or partners.

D SHOPPING

1 Mr Broughton always walks around his store once a day. Listen and decide which departments he visits, and in what order.

2 Listen again and answer the following questions or fill in the blanks.

1 '________ ________ I'm looking for ________ ________ ________ ________ wine bottles.'
2 'I'll go and get them.' What do you think are 'them'?
3 'I wonder ________ ________ ________ reach down that tin.'
4 'Would you like to try one on?' 'No ________ , ________ ________ ________ .'
5 'Yes, those look right. ________ ________ ________ ________ ?'
6 'I've ________ ________ in this store ________ 30 years.'

3 Street Markets

You are in a market. Some of the class are customers and some are market stall holders. Decide which role you want to play.

Stage 1

Stall holders: Choose the goods you are going to sell. Decide on prices for the goods you are selling. Remember, you want to make as much money as possible!

Customers: Find out what the stalls sell. Select two items you need and buy them as cheaply as possible. You may have to bargain.

Stage 2

Customers: You find that some of the goods are faulty, or that you can get them somewhere else more cheaply. Take them back to the stall you bought them from. Ask for a refund or replacement.

Stall holders: You want to avoid refunding any money, or replacing any goods. Be apologetic, but firm!

E

LEARNING TO LEARN

You don't only learn in the classroom. Make a list of the ways you can continue your language learning outside the classroom e.g.

1 Reading newspapers, advertisements etc.
2 Listening to the radio, television etc.

Compare your list with those of other students.

REVIEW

UNIT 1

PART 1 LANGUAGE REVIEW

Giving directions Describing places Suggestions Hopes and plans Offers and invitations

Multicultural Britain Eating out in Britain Unemployment

A

MULTICULTURAL BRITAIN

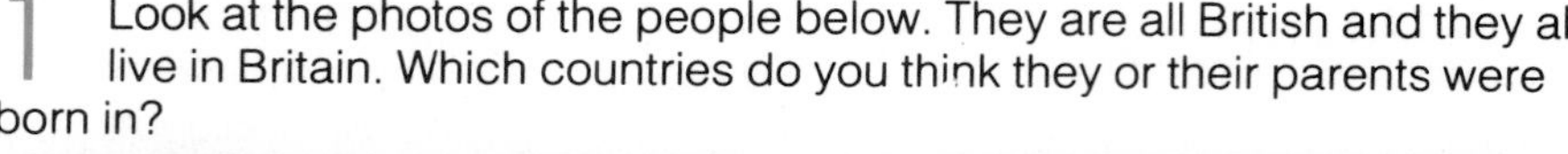

1 Look at the photos of the people below. They are all British and they all live in Britain. Which countries do you think they or their parents were born in?

2 The English language contains many words which have been 'borrowed' from other languages. Guess which language these words originally came from. Check in a dictionary if you're not sure of their meanings.

shampoo	bungalow	chutney	typhoon	restaurant	doolally
karate	jodhpurs	khaki	admiral	cafe	kiosk

B EATING OUT IN BRITAIN

1 Which country do you think these foods come from? Add other dishes to the list.

from . .	from . . .	from . .	from . .	from . .
curry	jambalaya	lasagna	chop suey	kebabs
. . . . .	. . . . .	. . . . .	. . . . .	. . . .

Asian Tandoori 73 St Mary St........................Cardiff 398913
Berni Steak House Citicenta St Mary St ....Cardiff 44511
Crumbs Salad Restaurant, Morgan Arc;
off St Mary St ....Cardiff 395007
Frontier Saloon: Steaks and a selection of Mexican food
7 High Street..Cardiff 20608
The Great British Burger 57 Queen St.............Cardiff 26833

JACKSONS
SUPERB INTERNATIONAL RESTAURANT
OPEN FOR LUNCHEONS AND EVENING DINNERS FROM TUESDAY TO SATURDAY ALSO AVAILABLE FOR PRIVATE FUNCTIONS
Racquets
CHOOSE FROM OUR EXTENSIVE A' LA CARTE OR SET MENU'S
THE RESTAURANT OVERLOOKS RACQUETS DISCOTHEQUE (SOUND PROOF GLASS) FOR WHICH THERE IS FREE ADMISSION FOR DINERS TO THE REST OF THE CLUB
CARDIFF 390851
WESTGATE STREET, CF1.

LA PIAF
FRENCH PROVINCIAL RESTAURANT
- SEATING UP TO 120
- PARTY BOOKINGS WELCOME
- FUNCTIONS/RECEPTIONS CATERED FOR
- IN HOUSE FRENCH CHEF
- FRIENDLY RELAXED ATMOSPHERE

AT THE GRAND HOTEL
5/7 WESTGATE ST CARDIFF
TELEPHONE 373257

Llandaff Restaurant Working St ....Cardiff 27211
Manuel's Restaurant 33 Charles St..................Cardiff 20650
Nino's Restaurant 40 St Mary St.......................Cardiff 20060
Piero's Restaurant 1 Senghenydd Rd ....Cardiff 20171
Pizza Land 8 High St.......................................Cardiff 21696
Riverside Cantonese Restaurant 44 Tudor St .Cardiff 372163
Savastano's Exquisite Italian Cuisine Access/Visa Welcome
302 North Rd..Cardiff 621018

DELICIOUS FOOD & GOOD VALUE
Sergio's Gourmet Restaurant
FULL FRENCH, ITALIAN & ENGLISH A LA CARTE MENU
OPEN 7 NIGHTS A WEEK AND FOR BOOKINGS AT LUNCHTIME
TRADITIONAL SUNDAY LUNCHES
WE CAN CATER FOR PARTIES OF UP TO 60
FULLY LICENSED
CARDIFF 33506
442C COWBRIDGE ROAD EAST VICTORIA PARK CARDIFF S.GLAM.

Sharif Restaurant, rear of 55 Charles St ....Cardiff 394767
Thai House Restaurant 23 High St ....Cardiff 387404
Wimpy 78 Queen St..Cardiff 41555

2 Britain is very much a multicultural society, particularly in large cities. This is reflected in the many different restaurants that cater for a wide variety of tastes.

Look at the map of Cardiff and the information on local restaurants. Decide on a restaurant that you would like to visit and give your partner directions on getting there. They should guess which restaurant you have chosen (some of the restaurants are in the same street; you may have to give more clues). Then form new pairs and give directions to a different restaurant.

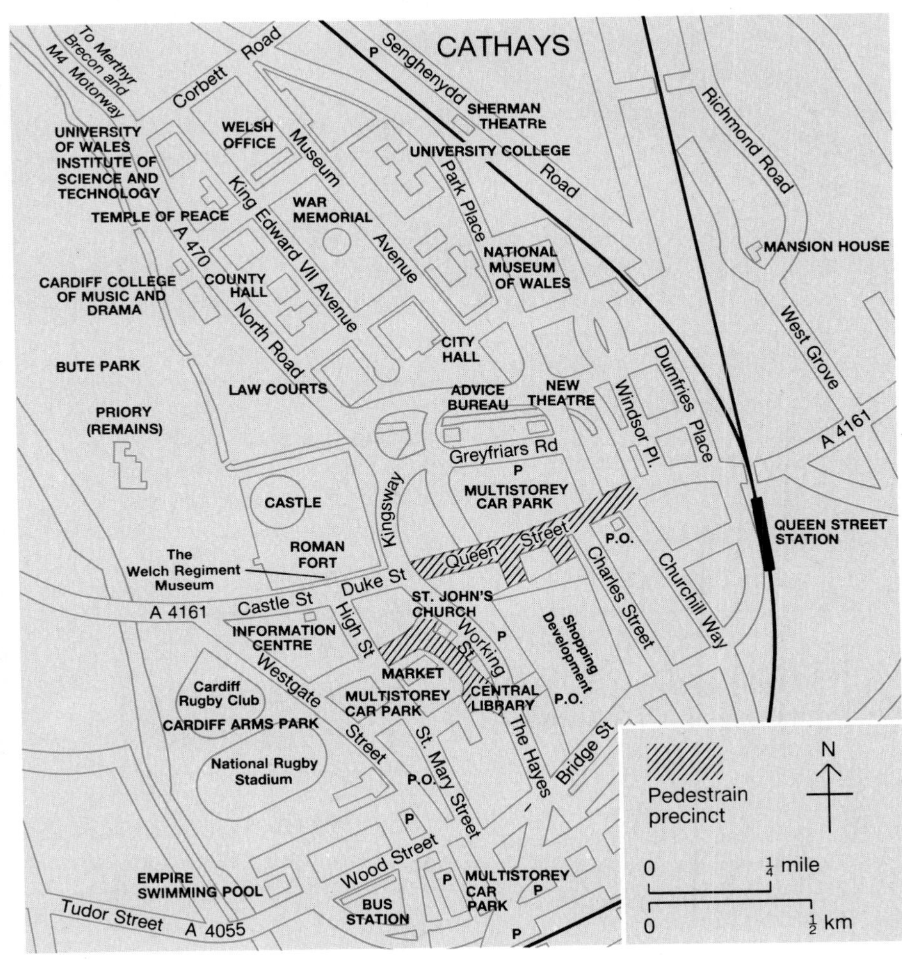

3 In a group make a list of the best restaurants in your town. Decide how to get there from your classrooms. Then either make a list of written instructions for the use of future students or write a short description of the restaurants, including reasons for your choice.

C

UNEMPLOYMENT

As in many other countries in the world, Britain has a lot of unemployment. People go to Job Centres to see what jobs are available and there is also a scheme that has been set up to help the long-term unemployed – the Jobclubs.

1 In small groups, imagine you are setting up a Jobclub. Make a list of suggestions for activities: think about how often you'll meet, who can join and what facilities you'll have. Tell the other groups your plans. If you think another group's ideas won't work, challenge them!

2 See how your ideas for a Jobclub correspond to what is available in Britain. Below is information from a leaflet 'An Introduction to Jobclub'. Match the questions to the answers.

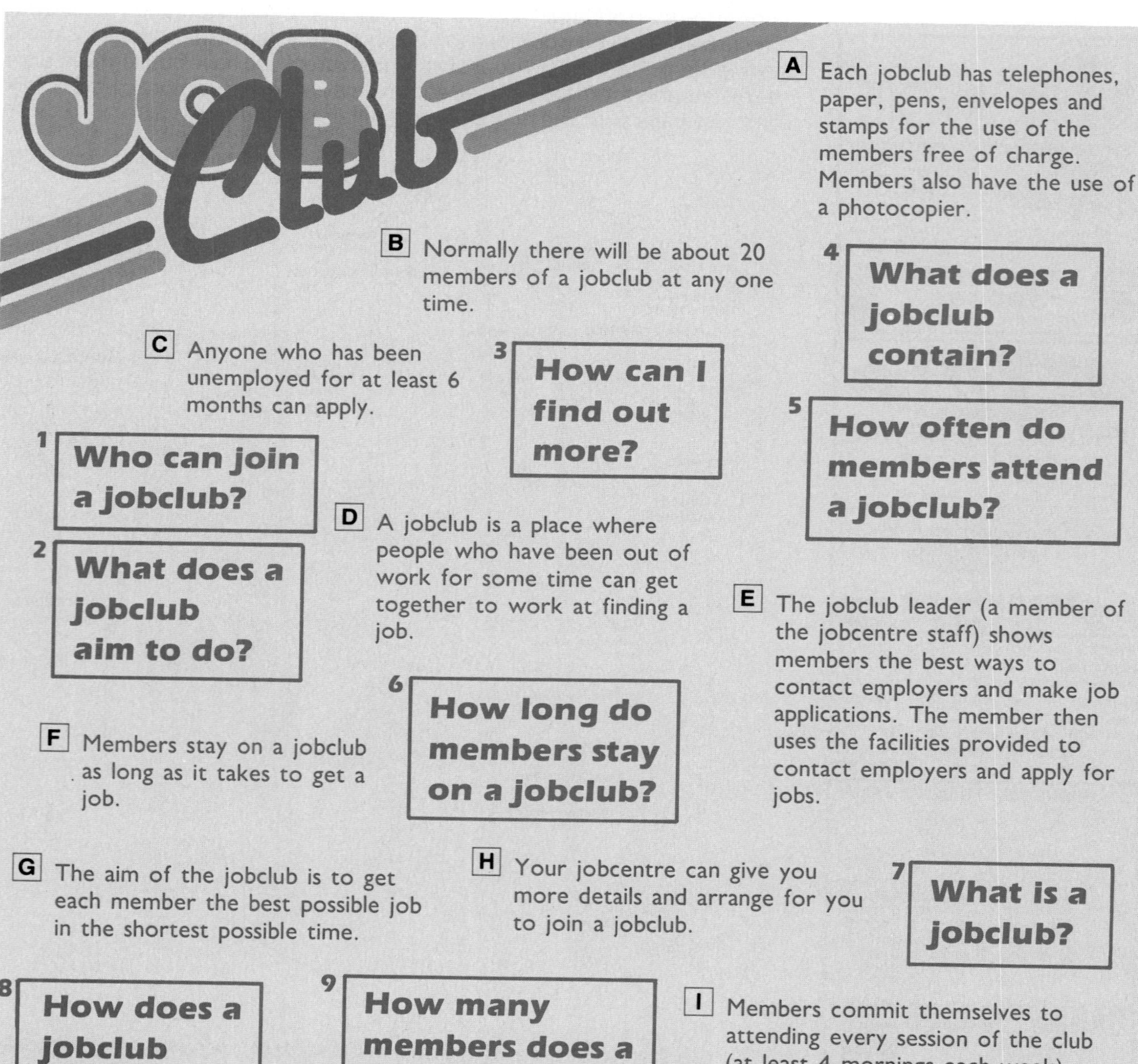

3 Work in groups of four. Choose a role card, study it and then play the role.

Mr/Ms Morgan

You lost your job in a hotel at the end of the holiday season and have been coming to the Jobclub for some time. You get on well with Mr/Ms McNeill and have got to know him/her well. You have missed the last two sessions of the club because you've had to stay at home looking after a sick child. You know the rule about regular attendance and must apologize to the Jobclub leader. You try to help the newcomer to settle down and make arrangements to see him/her and Mr/Ms McNeill at the end of the session.

Mr/Ms Dawkins

You are the Jobclub Leader and work there or at the Job Centre full-time. You teach members job-hunting techniques, e.g. how to present themselves at interview, by letter or on the phone. You are rather annoyed because one of the members has not been turning up regularly despite the rules. A new member comes to the club – ask him/her what he/she hopes to get out of joining the Jobclub.

Mr/Ms McNeill

You became redundant nine months ago after working for 15 years in a local engineering factory. You've been coming to the Jobclub for three weeks and have an interview the day after tomorrow in a new electronics factory. Ask the Jobclub leader for help with arrangements for the interview. Take the new member of the club in your care and introduce him/her to other people in the club. Invite him/her for a drink afterwards.

Mr/Ms Hayes

The Jobclub has suggested that you come to the club and you are eager to use all the facilities that are available. Tell the Jobclub leader what you are hoping to do in the future – you were only made redundant from your job in a travel agent's two weeks ago and are optimistic about the future. Other members of the club help you to settle in.

D LEARNING TO LEARN

Below is a list of the language items you have studied so far; the numbers in brackets refer to the units. Grade yourself according to how well you think you can now do these things.

√√√ very well
√√ quite well
√ need more practice

Can you . . .

greet people (Intro)?
introduce people to each other (Intro)?
ask for information (1)?
give directions (1)?
describe places (1)?
offer someone something (2)?
make requests (2)?
make suggestions (2)?
talk about your hopes and plans (2)?
make arrangements (2)?
complain (3)?
apologize (3)?

PART 2 PROJECT

Finding out about other countries

COMPARING COUNTRIES

You are going to find out as much as possible about another country from another student in the school.

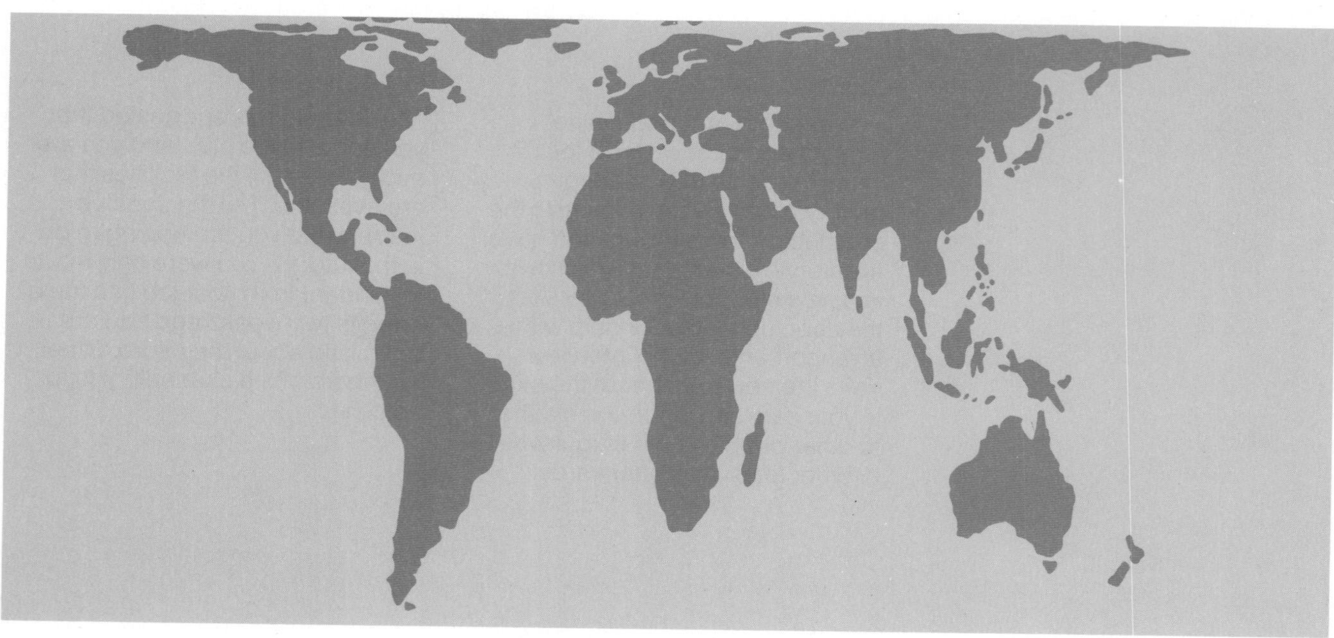

Stage 1 Preparation

1 Discuss with your teacher who you are going to interview. It could be someone in your own class, or the whole class might like to interview another class. Choose someone from a country which is as different as possible from your own.

2 Go to the nearest library and find out as much background information as possible about the country you have chosen, e.g.

Where is it?
How big is it?
What's the population?
What kind of government does it have?
What's the official religion?
What are the main products?
What are the main exports?

3 Now prepare a questionnaire. Write about five questions under each heading.

1. Family and marriage, e.g.
   Do young people live at home until they are married? ....
   ....
   ....
   ....
   ....
2. Social behaviour, e.g.
   How do you greet someone you don't know? ....
   ....
   ....
   ....
   ....
3. Food and meals, e.g.
   What time is the main meal of the day? ....
   ....
   ....
   ....
   ....
4. Education, e.g.
   When do children begin school? ....
   ....
   ....
   ....
   ....
5. Work and jobs, e.g.
   Where do people work? In towns or in the country? ....
   ....
   ....
   ....
   ....
6. Recreation and leisure, e.g.
   Is the theatre popular in your country? ....
   ....
   ....
   ....
   ....

Stage 2 The Interview

Ask your questions. Make notes of the answers.

Stage 3 The Report

Tell your class some of the things that surprised you or that you have learned. You may like to make a written report, tape-recording or video using all the information you now have about the country you chose.

Alternatively the whole class might like to make a wallchart including information about all the countries you have studied.

UNIT 4

THE WORLD ABOUT US

Describing things **Describing people**
Natural things **Personality**

A WHAT'S IT CALLED?

1 Listen to the two conversations at least once for each of the following tasks.

1 Who is talking to who? Where are they?

2 In conversation 1 the words *bolt* and *nut* are used with two different meanings. Which of the things in the pictures are bolts or nuts?

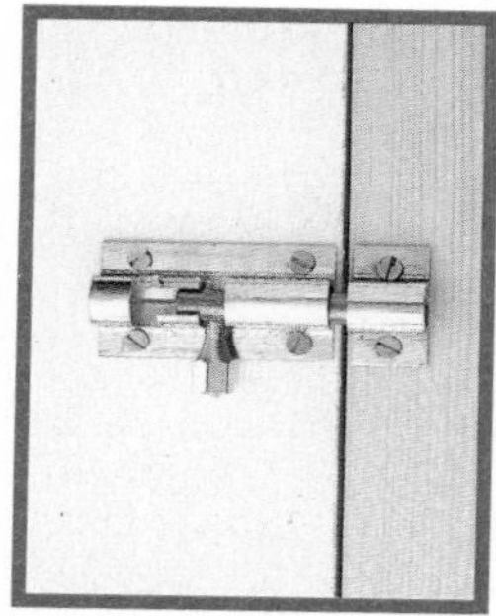

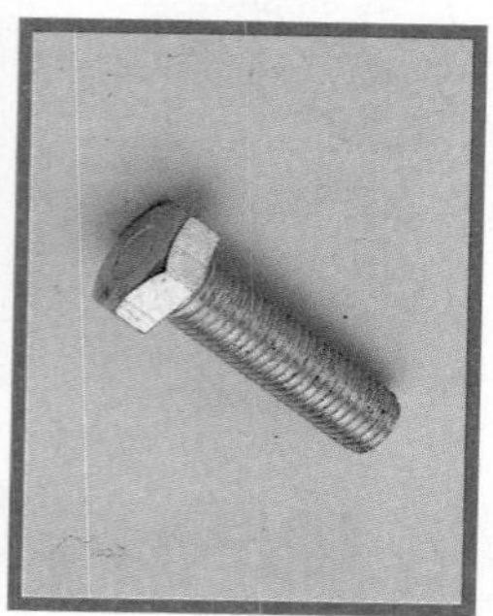

Do you know any more words with the same spelling but different meanings?

3 Fill in the first two columns of this chart.

	Object 1	**Object 2**	**Other words**
What shape is it?	. . . . . .	. . . . . .	. . . .
What colour is it?	. . . . . .	. . . . . .	. . . .
What's it made of?	. . . . . .	. . . . . .	. . . .
What size is it? (How big is it?)	. . . . . .	. . . . . .	. . . .

4 Now make a note of any extra information about the objects, e.g. what parts has it got?

Object 1 ....

Object 2 ....

5 What are the objects?

2 Use the information in the chart to write a short description of each object. Notice this word order:

It's a (size), (shape), (colour) object with (extra information), which is made of (materials) and is used for (use). It's like a . . .

3 Think of more words to describe shape, size, colour etc. Write the words in the third column in the chart.

4 Work in groups of four. One person thinks of an object. The other people in the group try to guess what the object is by asking simple questions, e.g.

Is it big?	Yes, it is.
Is it used for cooking?	No, it isn't.

B COLOURS

1 Most colours are described in terms of these basic ones:

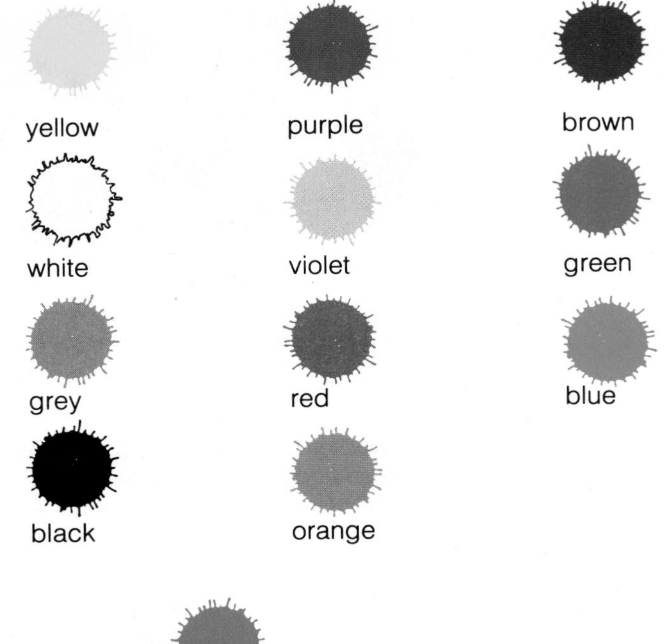

Note: a blue-green colour=green with some blue

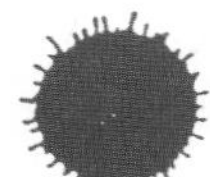

a reddish-brown colour = ...   a silvery-white colour = ...

Discuss some of the colours around you. Do you all agree?

2 Work in groups. Read the list of colours and discuss where the name of the colour comes from (a rock, a fruit, a plant, etc.) Then discuss them in terms of their basic colours, and try to think of things which might have the colour.

primrose	magnolia	cream	ginger
lime	charcoal	apricot	burgundy
lavender	emerald	gold	copper
plum	ebony	peach	chestnut
ruby	tan	rust	
silver	olive	lemon	

C

MALAYSIAN FRUIT

1 An object is usually described in terms of size, shape and colour, but sometimes information about texture, smell or taste is important.

Read these descriptions and underline the words which describe the smell, taste and texture of the fruit.

1 A *rambutan* is one of the most popular fruits in Malaysia. It smells sweet and fresh and is very juicy. It is round, red and hairy-skinned. Inside is a white jelly-like fruit with a stone in the middle.

2 A *mangosteen* is a fruit with a thick purplish-black skin and large seeds which are covered by a sweet white flesh. It smells fresh and is very soft. It is an attractive fruit with a delicious taste.

3 A *langsat* has a thin yellow skin. It is round and has large seeds surrounded by white or transparent segments of flesh. It can taste a bit sour or even bitter and it has no smell.

4 A *ciku* is a very soft and tender fruit which won't keep very long. It is delicious, sweet and juicy. It is brownish in colour, both inside and out, and it is the size and shape of an egg.

5 A *durian* is described as the king of the fruits and it can be quite expensive. It has a very hard, spiky skin which has to be opened by a sharp knife to reveal the rolls of fairly solid flesh. It has a strong, distinctive smell, lovely and fresh to some, disgusting to others. It tastes sweet, creamy and soft.

Now write the words you have underlined in appropriate columns as below, and add any more words you can think of. Has your partner got the same tastes?

SMELL	TASTE	TEXTURE

2 Describe your favourite fruit or vegetable to another student. Use words to describe shape, colour, smell, taste and texture. Your partner must try to identify the fruit or vegetable.

D

DESCRIBE YOURSELF

1 Imagine you are going for a walk through a forest. Use your imagination to describe your walk and all the things you see and do on the walk.

1 You are in a *forest*. It's . . . . .
2 You are on a *path*. It's . . . . .
3 You are looking for a *key*. It's . . . . .
4 You see a *bear* in your path. It's . . . . . so you . . . . .
5 You come to some *water*. It's . . . . .
6 You *cross* the water by . . . . .
7 You are on the *other side of the water*. It's . . . . .
8 You come to a *building*. It's . . . . . and you . . . . .

2 [cassette] D1 was an exercise in describing yourself psychologically. Now look at the language for describing people physically. Listen and read this description, and the list of aspects.

ASPECTS	
Face and body age complexion build height facial features	She must have been in her mid-twenties. She was tall and slim, with long blonde hair, and although she could have been a model – her statistics were right – she wasn't really what you'd call beautiful or even attractive. As I've said, she was well-proportioned, with a peaches and cream complexion, but she was rather thin-lipped and her cold blue eyes seemed to look right through you.
Clothes	She always wore the most fashionable clothes, and although you couldn't say they didn't suit her, somehow the whole effect jarred, as if she was wearing them through duty, not comfort.
Expression facial and body	She would stand very straight and tall and direct her piercing gaze in a way that almost defied anyone to approach her.
Character & habits emotional physical mental	It was only when you studied her for any length of time that you'd notice her hand creep up to play nervously with a lock of hair, or the occasional flicker of a smile at the corner of her mouth. Once I saw her laugh, really laugh long and hard, and then her whole face lit up and she was quite beautiful.

3 In pairs consider each of the aspects listed in D2. Think of as many words as you can to describe each aspect. Then compare your list with other students'.

4 Now write a 'portrait' of yourself. Try to include as many aspects, psychological as well as physical, as you can.

E

WHO ARE YOU?

1 Work by yourself and answer the following questions. Write the first answer that comes into your head.

1. Who are you?
2. What motivates you?
3. How do you know that someone likes you?
4. How do you show someone you like them?
5. What makes you feel secure?

2 The answers to the questions in E1 are used to decide which 'colour personality' people fit into. Below are two of the seven colours of the spectrum attributed to personality types. Discuss if anyone in the class fits them.

YELLOW PERSON

Identifies with change, novelty and new experience. Will always have a new/novel way of seeing things. Good debater, as he/she can see both sides of an argument. Love – prefers variety of expression and sometimes partners.
Positive aspects: Offers new points of view on existing arguments. Intellectual wit. Good arbitrator. Keen investigator/explorer.
Negative aspects: Fixed attitudes that are outside normal social confines. Sarcastic and pessimistic about life, friends, and the future. Unable to commit himself/herself to action or relationships.

BLUE PERSON

Identifies with order, authority and systems of control. Paternal in attitudes to others. Sees other people as children to be looked after. Needs to keep the status-quo and is threatened by chaos. Love – expressed through paternal caring.
Positive aspects: Father/mother figure within society. Very often in politics, committees and rule-making bodies. Finds fulfillment in caring for others.
Negative aspects: Fixed in thoughts and attitudes. Emotionally repressed with deep distrust of people who show their feelings easily.

F

LEARNING TO LEARN

1 How did you learn English? Write down three things that helped you. Now compare your list with your neighbour's. Are they the same?

2 Rank the following ways of studying in their order of importance for you.

- ☐ studying regularly
- ☐ talking to other students
- ☐ talking to English people
- ☐ going to classes
- ☐ studying on your own
- ☐ studying when you feel like it
- ☐ reading a lot
- ☐ listening to English radio, TV, songs
- ☐ writing everything down
- ☐ getting involved with the language-learning group
- ☐ working in a language lab

UNIT 5

SIMILARITIES & DIFFERENCES

Comparison **Describing processes**

Statistics **Developing world** **Chewing gum**

A DEVELOPING COUNTRIES

1 This table gives basic information about 20 different countries and summarizes their level of development in 1984.

How many of the countries can you find on a map of the world?

	Country	A	B	C	D	E
1	Burkina Faso	$160	1.8	83	11	5
2	Tanzania	$210	3.4	83	14	66
3	India	$260	2.3	74	25	36
4	China	$310	1.4	62	22	—
5	Kenya	$310	4.0	79	18	40
6	Zambia	$470	3.2	68	48	39
7	Indonesia	$540	2.3	60	25	62
8	Morocco	$670	2.4	53	43	28
9	Egypt	$720	2.6	51	23	44
10	Nigeria	$730	2.8	56	30	—
11	Brazil	$1,720	2.3	41	72	76
12	Malaysia	$1,980	2.4	50	31	60
13	Mexico	$2,040	2.9	39	69	76
14	Venezuela	$3,410	3.3	20	85	82
15	USSR	?	0.9	17	66	99
16	Italy	$6,420	0.3	13	71	98
17	UK	$8,570	(.)	2	92	99
18	Japan	$10,630	0.9	13	76	99
19	W. Germany	$11,130	−0.1	4	86	99
20	USA	$15,390	1.0	2	74	99

A = GNP (Gross National Product) per head (US dollars)
B = Population growth rate (%)
C = Labour force in agriculture (%)
D = Urban population (%)
E = Adult literacy rate (%)

2 Divide into five groups. Each group look at one set of figures, and answer these questions about your figures.

1 Which countries have a higher . . . . . than India?
2 Which country has the lowest . . . . . ?
3 Which countries have a similar . . . . . ?
4 Which countries differ a great deal in their . . . . . ?
5 Which countries have a low . . . . . compared with Japan?

3 Now re-form into five new groups, with a member from each of the first groups. Share your information.

1 Which are the richest and the poorest countries?
2 Is there any relationship between the different sets of figures?
3 What problems do you think the poorer countries have?
4 Is there anything about the figures that surprises you?

4 In 1980, Willi Brandt, former Chancellor of West Germany, produced a report for the EEC on the relations between developed and developing countries. The message of the report is clear: all countries must work together to resolve their differences and co-operate to overcome the major threats to mankind. Below is a cartoon which comments on the situation described in the Brandt Report.

In small groups, discuss what the cartoon below means to you.

B UP A GUM TREE!

1 Before you listen to a passage about the collection of the gum used to make chewing gum, answer these questions.

1 A group of trees can be called a wood. What other words do you know to describe a group of trees?

2 Label the different types of knives below. Choose from:

penknife carving-knife dagger machete flick-knife breadknife

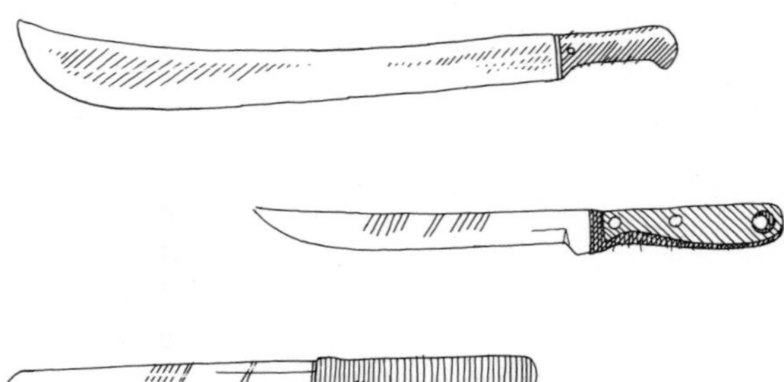

3 In small groups, think of as many words as you can, in one minute, which are associated with water transport. Compare your lists.

2 Now listen to the passage and complete the flow chart on the next page. There is one box for each stage of the process.

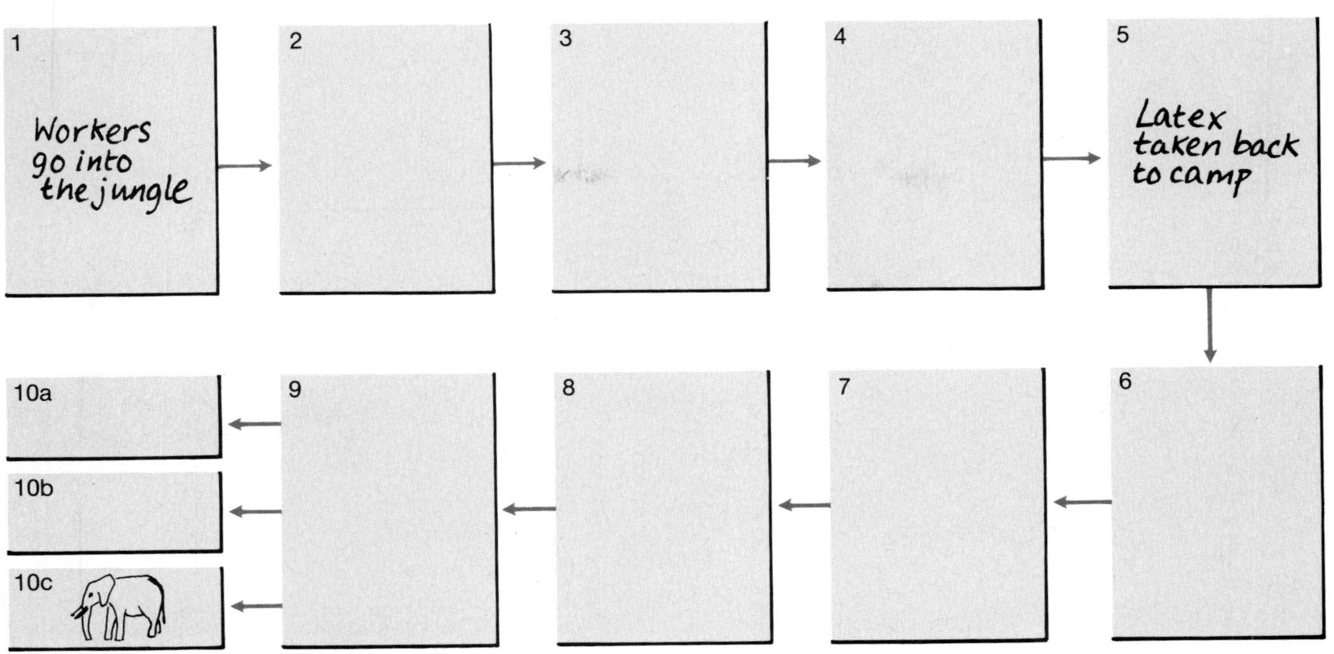

3 Write out the steps in the processing of latex in complete sentences using these words:

First After Then Next Following this Finally

C

BY GUM!

1 Below, in jumbled order, are the stages in the process of making chewing gum. Match them with the pictures on the next page. The first one has been done for you.

- [ ] Gum base ground and melted
- [ ] Rolling and sheeting
- [ ] Inspection
- [ ] Mixing and blending
- [ ] Raw materials delivered to refinery
- [ ] Purification by centrifuge
- [1] Collection of gum base raw materials
- [ ] Other ingredients added
- [ ] Despatch
- [ ] Wrapping

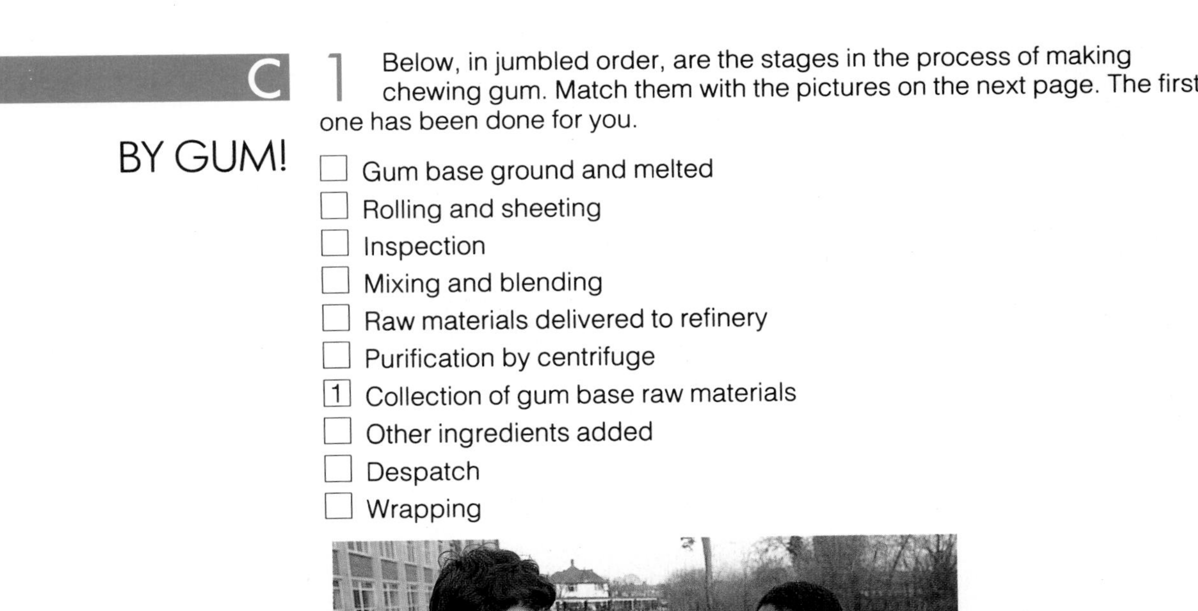

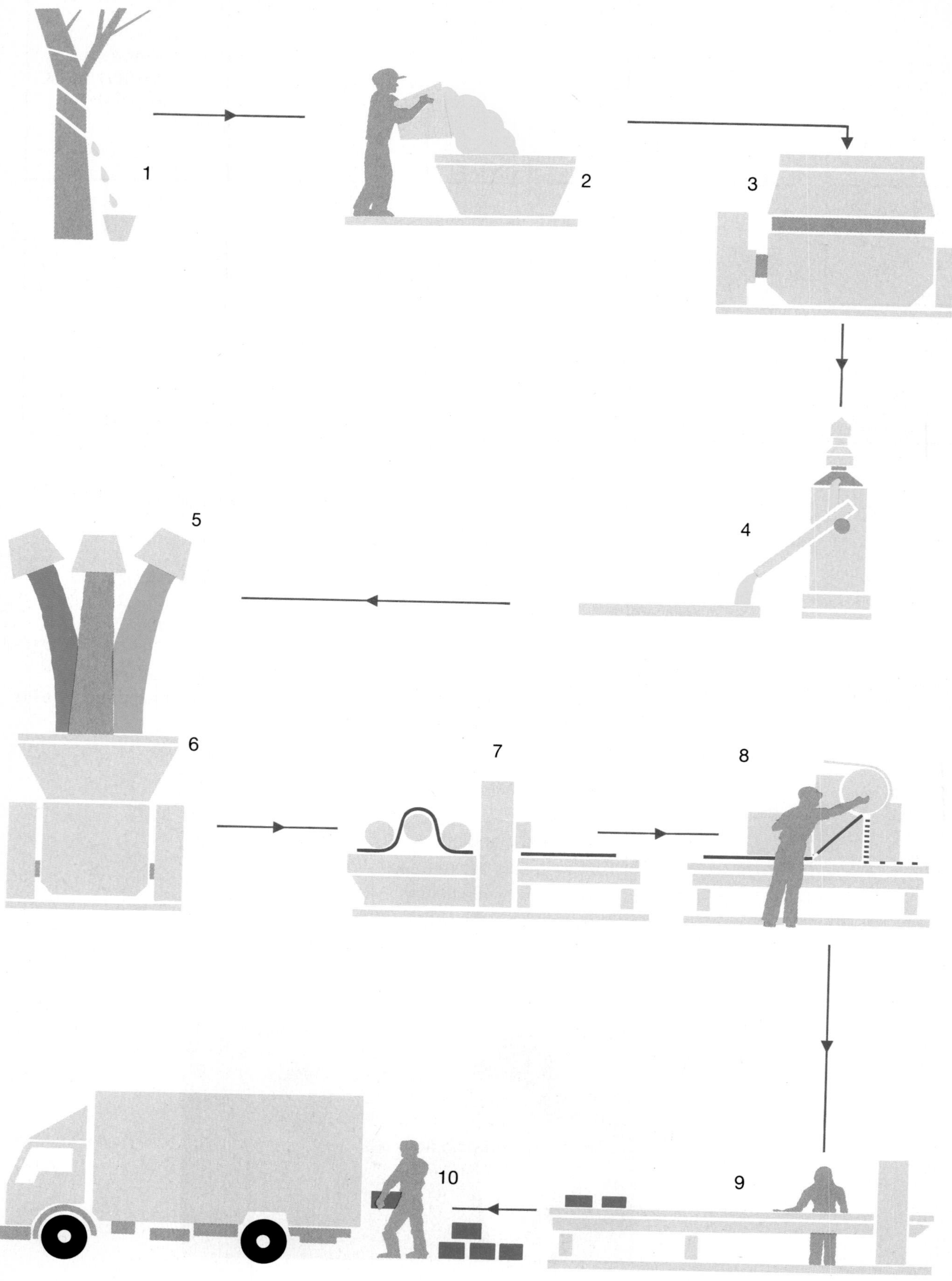
1
2
3
4
5
6
7
8
9
10

2 Imagine that yesterday you went to a chewing gum factory to see gum being made.

1 In pairs, ask and answer about what you saw. Use the information in C1 and the verbs in the box below to help you.

were added
were delivered
was despatched
was ground and melted
was inspected
was mixed and blended
was purified
was rolled and made into sheets
was wrapped

2 Write a report about what happened. Use *then*, *next*, *after*, or *finally* to connect your sentences. Begin:

'First the raw materials were delivered . . .'

D INVENTIONS

What do you hate doing most? The drawings show the inventions of two children who were asked to design a machine to do the job that they hated most – walking the dog!

Design a machine to do your worst job for you. Explain your invention to other students.

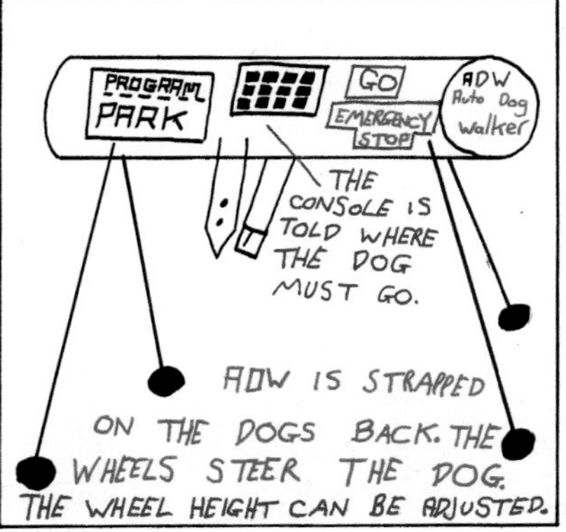

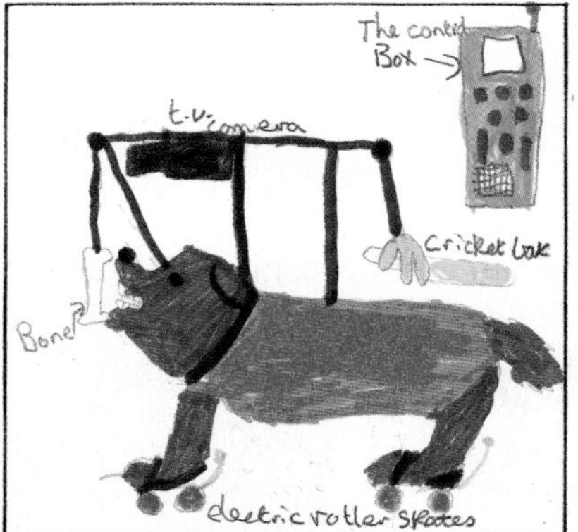

Personal valet machine

Waking-up machine

Keeping the baby happy machine

Put-you-to-sleep machine

E LEARNING TO LEARN

Would the following three suggestions help you to learn? Discuss with the other students.

1 Set yourself realistic targets and a time limit to reach them, e.g. using a new language point in some practical way, preferably outside the classroom, by the end of the week.

2 At the end of the day read through what you have done in class, and every so often review the work you did in previous classes.

3 Keep a language-learning diary and note down:

– language-learning activities you have done, e.g. "listened to the radio, understood main points" or "eavesdropped on a conversation in a cafe, able to understand most of it and realized they were cross with each other"

– problem areas you have encountered, e.g. "giving up reading the newspaper, even with the help of a dictionary it was too difficult"

REMEMBERING THE PAST

Describing past actions and events

Customs and beliefs   Myths

A

THE GOOD OLD DAYS?

1 Think of as many gadgets/appliances as you can for heating or keeping things warm, e.g. radiator, electric blanket, oven. Compare your lists and sort the words into families or categories.

2 Listen to two old ladies reminiscing about their early lives, and make notes about how they used to manage without the modern conveniences listed below.

Now	**Then**
washing machines	. . . . . .
vacuum cleaners	. . . . . .
radiators	. . . . . .
delivery vans	. . . . . .

3 Discuss what you think life used to be like for the people in the photographs.

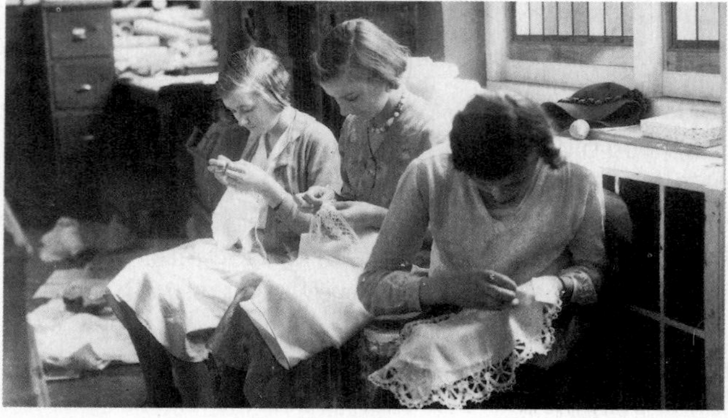

B STILLS

1 Discuss the photos. What *was happening* just before the photo was taken? What *happened* after?

2 Imagine your photo album, or your collection of old family photos. Imagine you are looking through them. Stop when you find one you like. 'See' it very clearly. 'See' the positions of the people in the photo, and the surroundings.

- What were you doing when the photo was taken?
- What had you done before the photo was taken?
- What did you do after the photo was taken?

In groups, tell the story of your photo.

C

TRADITION AND CHANGE

1 The following extract is taken from *Things Fall Apart* by Chinua Achebe, a novel which describes the change in the life of an African village after the arrival of the first European missionaries. The extract describes how Okonkwo has to leave his village for offending traditional beliefs.

Before you begin, discuss what you think those beliefs were.

Look quickly through the passage. Were you right?

What had Okonkwo wanted to become before he left the village?

> Okonkwo and his family worked very hard to plant a new farm. But it was like beginning life anew without the vigour and enthusiasm of youth, like learning to become left-handed in old age. Work no longer had for him the pleasure it used to have, and when there was no work to do he sat in a silent half-sleep.
>
> His life had been ruled by a great passion – to become one of the lords of the clan. That had been his life-spring. And he had all but achieved it. Then everything had been broken. He had been cast out of his clan, like a fish on to a dry, sandy beach, panting. Clearly his personal god or *chi* was not made for great things. A man could not rise above the destiny of his *chi*. The saying of the elders was not true – that if a man said yea his *chi* also affirmed. Here was a man whose *chi* said nay despite his own affirmation.
>
> 27

2 Now read the passage again and answer these questions.

1 What sort of work did he do?
2 How did his feelings towards his work change after he had left the village?
3 What did the elders say about the *chi*?
4 Did Okonkwo agree with them?
5 Have you guessed what the meaning of the word *chi* is?

3 Find words in the passage which mean the same as . . .

1 energy
2 strong interest
3 strong feeling
4 community
5 belonging to a particular person
6 end decided by someone or something else
7 agreed
8 yes
9 no

4 What do you know about life in Africa 100 years ago? How did Africa and Europe differ? Find out more about Africa and Chinua Achebe in your local library.

D

THE FORBIDDEN FRUIT – AN AFRICAN FOLK STORY

1 Listen to the story and make notes, using the sequencing markers below. Re-write the story in your own words, using your notes.

In the beginning . . .
Then . . .
So . . .
And then . . .

At first . . .
But one day . . .
She therefore . . .
To begin with . . .
But after a time . . .

However . . .
This . . .

2 Work in groups. Think of a similar type of story. Make some notes about it, making sure it is clearly sequenced, but don't 'write' the story. Then tell your story to another group.

E

LEARNING TO LEARN

Make a list of all the things the class have read since they last met. What was the reason for reading them? Did this affect the way you read them?

REVIEW UNIT 2

PART 1 LANGUAGE REVIEW

Describing people and places Describing past actions and events Comparing places

Britain: people, places and accents

A GRANDAD!

1 Make a list of ten words to describe one of your grandparents. In pairs or groups tell each other about your grandparent.

2 Listen to Steve's description of his grandfather, and put the following events in the appropriate order.

1 He left school at 14.
2 He went all over England on barges.
3 All his mates called him Skip.
4 We lived in a two-up two-down.
5 He let the kids run around the block for tuppence.
6 They never locked the front door.
7 The girls got him one of those kissograms.
8 He gave us money.

3 Listen again and complete this form with details about Steve's grandad.

Name ....
Religion ....
Age now ....
Home town ....
Age left school ....
Jobs: 1 ....
2 ....
3 ....

4 As you listen this time, make a list of words that describe Steve's grandad for you. Compare your lists with other students'. Are they the same? Explain your choice of words if necessary.

B

A TALE OF TWO TOWNS

1 Do you know a town which is/was dependent on one main industry? Tell each other about it. Then listen to the description of two towns on the tape. What was the main industry in each one?

2 Match the words below with the right pictures and, as you listen again, decide which pictures belong to Liverpool and which to the Welsh mining town.

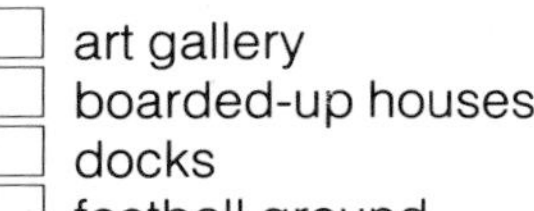

- [ ] art gallery
- [ ] boarded-up houses
- [ ] docks
- [ ] football ground
- [ ] grey slate roofs
- [ ] pits
- [ ] ribbon development
- [ ] town centre
- [ ] valley and hills

1

2

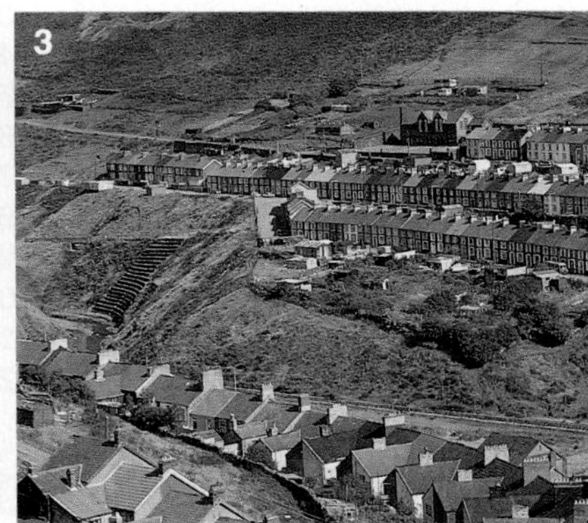
3

4

5

6

7

8

9

3 As you listen this time, make notes on the similarities and differences between the two towns. How are they different? How are they similar, and why? How do they compare with the town you thought of in B1?

C

TWO TALES

1 Make up two short stories using the following two groups of words.

1 trolley-bus, pole, conductor, tomatoes, inexperienced, crashed, chauvinist, traffic jam

2 crane operator, rig, lifeboat, guy, engine, hobnailed boots, spark plugs, Texan

Exchange your stories.

2 Listen to the two stories and decide which of the events below belong to the lifeboat story and which to the trolley-bus story.

1 The alarm went off.
2 Rod and his mate laughed.
3 The booms came off the wires.
4 A truck with tomatoes tried to pass.
5 The driver got out of the trolley-bus.
6 They realized they didn't know how to start it.
7 The passengers got fed up and left.
8 The superintendent ordered an 'abandon rig' drill.
9 They smashed the spark plugs to avoid getting into trouble.
10 The bus ran backwards and hit a van.
11 Rod and the chief derrickman went straight to their lifeboat.
12 There was a complete traffic jam.

3 Listen again and put the events of each story in the right order.

D

WHERE ARE THEY FROM?

Listen to four extracts from the listening passages in this unit. They demonstrate the different accents of the four speakers. Which part of Britain do the four men come from?

1 Steve comes from . . . . .

2 Leon comes from . . . . .

3 Dave comes from . . . . .

4 Rod comes from . . . . .

E

LEARNING TO LEARN

Below is a list of the language items you have studied in Units 4–6; the numbers in brackets refer to the units. Grade yourself according to how well you think you can now do these things.

√√√ very well
√√ quite well
√ need more practice

Can you . . .

describe things (4) ?
describe people (4) ?
make comparisons (5) ?
describe a process (5) ?
report a process (5) ?
talk about the past (6) ?

PART 2 SIMULATION

DALELAKEMOOR

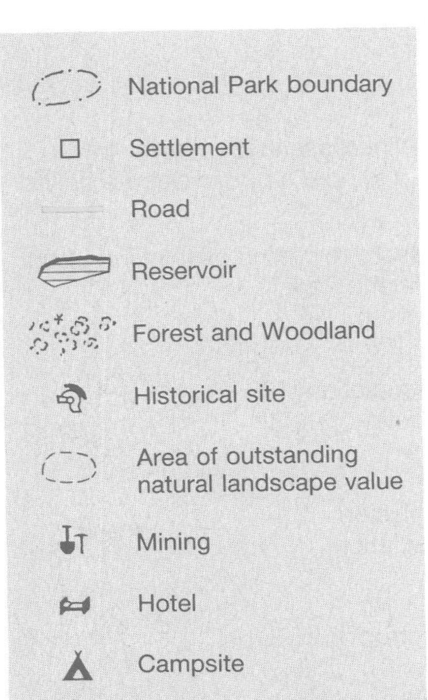

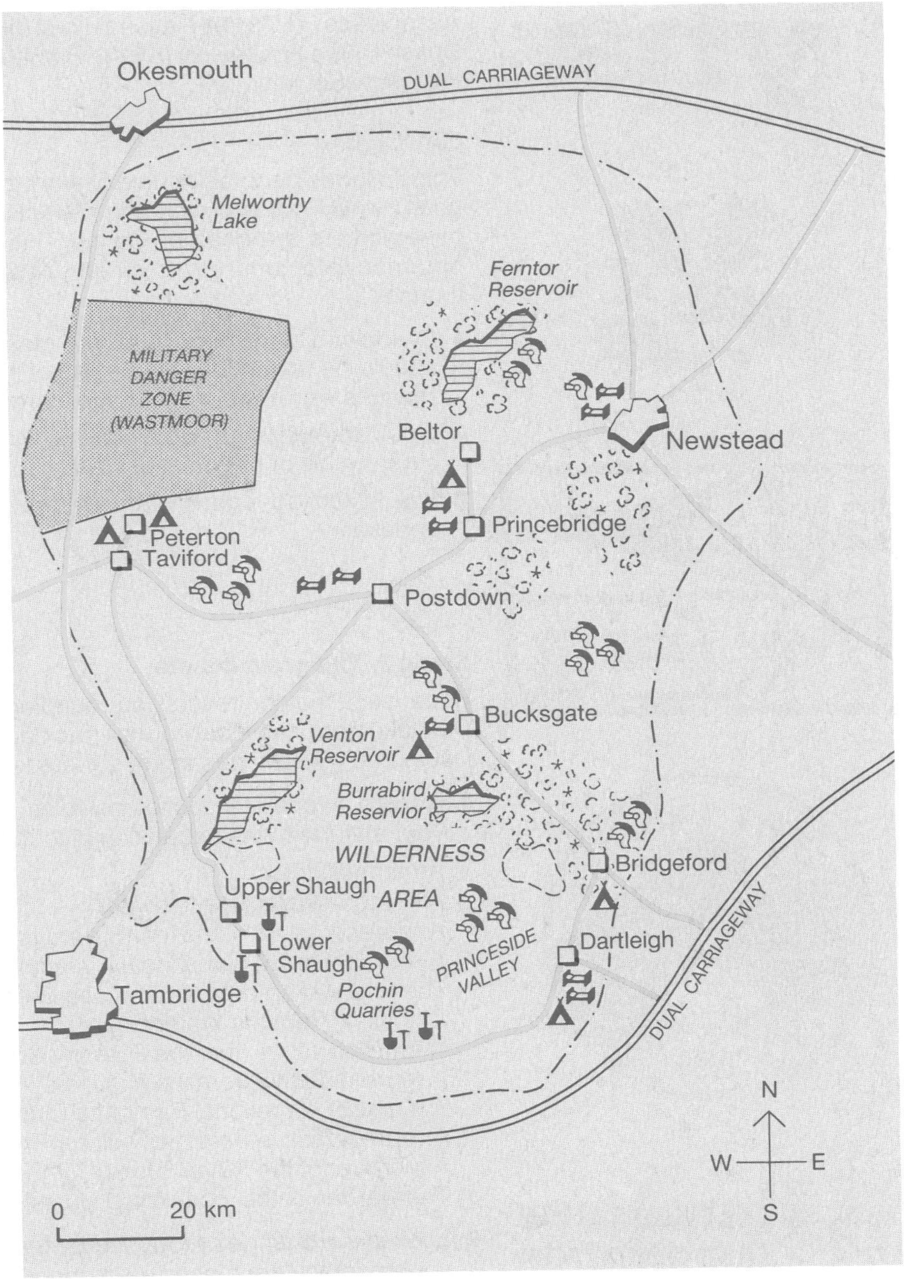

Stage 1 Preparation

Dalelakemoor is the largest and most visited National Park in the UK. Many of the problems now faced by both residents and visitors stem from the vast increase in tourism in recent years.

Look at the map in pairs. Decide what problems may face Dalelakemoor and other National Parks.

Stage 2 The problem

People who are concerned about the Park fall roughly into two groups:

GROUP A

This is the 'anti-expansion' group. It includes the Royal Society for the Protection of Birds (RSPB), County Naturalist Clubs, the Youth Hostel Association (YHA), the National Trust (NT), Camping and Caravan Clubs, the British Horse Society (BHS), the Rambler's Association, and the local Historical Society.

GROUP B

This includes people who live or work in the Park: farmers, restaurant and hotel owners, forestry workers, Water Board officials, the military, quarry and mine workers, the local Job Centre. This group would like to encourage more opportunity for jobs, e.g. in forestry, quarrying, farming and, particularly, tourism.

1 Divide into two groups. Group A makes a list of all the reasons why there should be restrictions on the use of the Park. Group B makes a list of reasons why it is better to have more people and more jobs.
2 One person from Group A pairs up with someone from Group B. Each one explains his or her point of view.
3 [cassette] Listen to the radio interview. How many of your points are made by the speakers?

Stage 3 The great debate

Because of the controversy surrounding the increase in tourism in Dalelakemoor, the local council has decided to hold a public debate on the issue. You will take part in the debate.

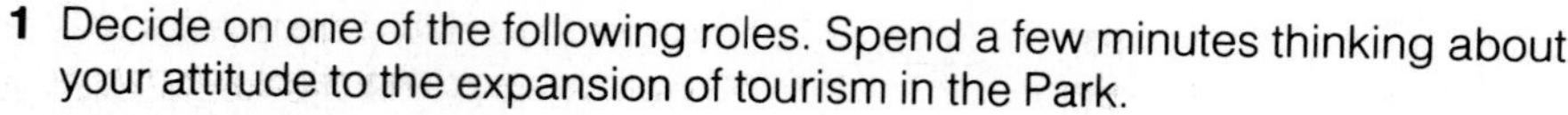

1 Decide on one of the following roles. Spend a few minutes thinking about your attitude to the expansion of tourism in the Park.

   An army officer
   A camp or caravan site owner
   A representative of the local Farmers' Association
   A representative of the local Historical Society
   The regional co-ordinator for Job Centres
   An official from the Water Board
   A representative from the Forestry Commission
   A representative from the Hoteliers' Association
   A member of the local Rambling Club
   A representative from the National Trust
   A member of the Royal Society for the Protection of Birds
   The warden of the local Youth Hostel

2 Look at the changes proposed by the local council on the next page. Do you think they are a good idea or not?

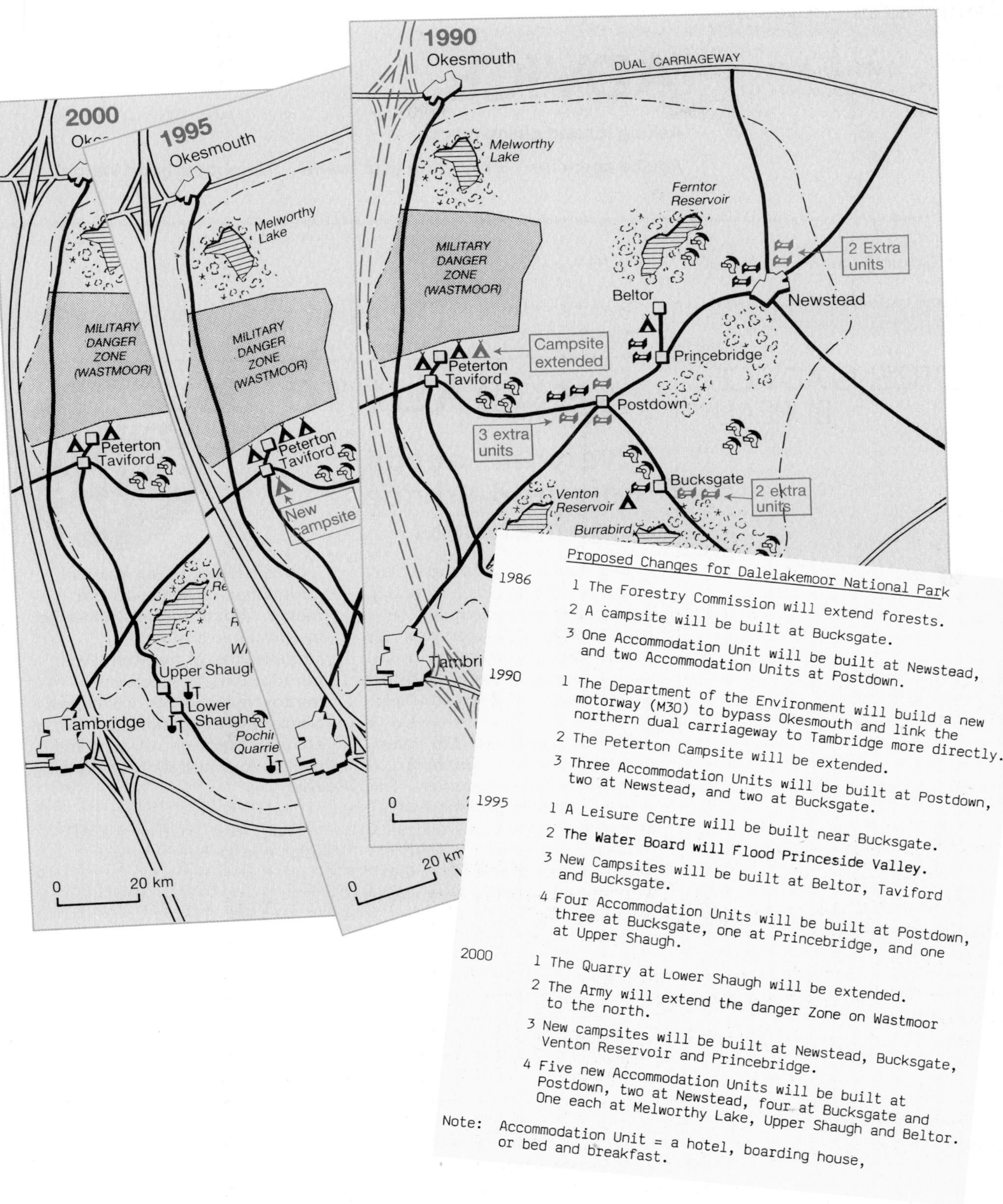

Proposed Changes for Dalelakemoor National Park

1986
1 The Forestry Commission will extend forests.
2 A campsite will be built at Bucksgate.
3 One Accommodation Unit will be built at Newstead, and two Accommodation Units at Postdown.

1990
1 The Department of the Environment will build a new motorway (M30) to bypass Okesmouth and link the northern dual carriageway to Tambridge more directly.
2 The Peterton Campsite will be extended.
3 Three Accommodation Units will be built at Postdown, two at Newstead, and two at Bucksgate.

1995
1 A Leisure Centre will be built near Bucksgate.
2 The Water Board will Flood Princeside Valley.
3 New Campsites will be built at Beltor, Taviford and Bucksgate.
4 Four Accommodation Units will be built at Postdown, three at Bucksgate, one at Princebridge, and one at Upper Shaugh.

2000
1 The Quarry at Lower Shaugh will be extended.
2 The Army will extend the danger Zone on Wastmoor to the north.
3 New campsites will be built at Newstead, Bucksgate, Venton Reservoir and Princebridge.
4 Five new Accommodation Units will be built at Postdown, two at Newstead, four at Bucksgate and One each at Melworthy Lake, Upper Shaugh and Beltor.

Note: Accommodation Unit = a hotel, boarding house, or bed and breakfast.

3 The debate is chaired by a representative from the local council. Be prepared to speak for a minute or two on your point of view.

UNIT 7

ADVICE

Asking for and giving advice

Advice agencies   Protecting your home   'Neighbourhood Watch'

A

CITIZENS ADVICE BUREAU

1 Read the leaflet. Is the Citizens Advice Bureau a general or a specialist advice bureau?

TALK TO US

Citizens Advice Bureau

Everyone needs help and advice sometimes.

Even really bright people can't know everything. Each year our laws, rules and regulations become even more complex. It's hardly surprising so many of us can't understand them. And that's where your local CAB can help.

It's their job to listen to your questions and do everything possible to find the answers. Of course they take pride in being able to help with really difficult problems. To some the CAB is the last resort. But a lot of their work concerns people's requests for information and advice on everyday matters.

We're asked for all kinds of information. A difficult legal matter. Where responsibilities lie in consumer disputes. Complexities of the Rent Acts. Introductions to specialists. Improvement grants. Taxes and claims. Housing and rates. Social security. Marriage, divorce and family. And just about everything else!

That's how your local CAB helps you to help yourself.

Ask us.

A few things your CAB can help with:

Housing	Consumer queries	The family
Social security	Disablement benefits and aids	Medical treatment
Employment problems	Pensions	Education
Redundancy	The Law	HP agreements

2 Look at the box in the leaflet. Where could the CAB send people who had these problems?

3 Find out if there is a CAB in the town you are in. Ask them for more information about their work. Is there anything like the CAB in your country?

B

ASKING FOR AND GIVING ADVICE

1 Listen to two people talking about their problems. Fill in the information below.

	Conversation 1	**Conversation 2**
Place	....	....
Relationship of people	....	....
Problem	....	....
Advice given	....	....

2 Listen to the two conversations again and make a note of the phrases used to ask for, give, accept and refuse advice. Write the phrases in columns and think of more phrases to add to each column.

Asking	Giving	Accepting	Refusing

Now look at the phrases in your columns and decide whether they are (1) formal or (2) friendly or (3) tentative/delicate. Some of them would fit into two or more categories. Try saying them to each other in formal or friendly or tentative ways.

3 Work in pairs. Ask your partner for advice: you don't know what to do on Saturday/at the end of the course/next year/about improving your English. You can accept the advice your partner gives you or not.

Remember: when you refuse advice, you should give a reason:
'I'd like to go to the disco, but I haven't enough money.'

4 Work in groups of four. Choose one problem each. Take it in turns to present your problems to the 'advice panel'.

1 You are a teenager, just arrived in town and looking for a job.
2 You have just been made redundant. Your company gave you a lump sum of £3000. You'd like advice on how to invest it.
3 Your child is about to start at a school which has compulsory school uniform. You want your child to go there, but you can't afford the uniform.
4 You bought a microwave but the door doesn't shut properly. The shop refuses either to refund the money or to replace the microwave.

C

WATCH OUT! THERE'S A THIEF ABOUT!

1 Listen – for some authoritative advice – to a policeman giving advice to a householder who is worried that thieves may break into the house while she's away. Look at the pictures from the leaflet *Protect Your Home* as you listen.

1 Tick the pictures which illustrate the points mentioned by the policeman.
2 Make notes on the two additional pieces of advice which are not illustrated.

A practised thief knows all the ways into a house.
Without realizing it,
we often make things easy for him.

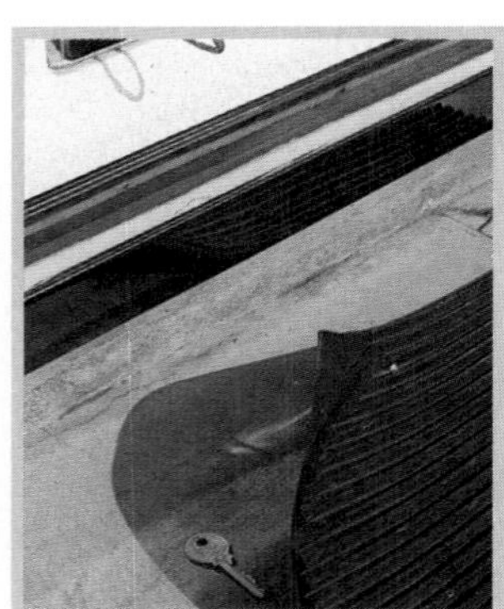

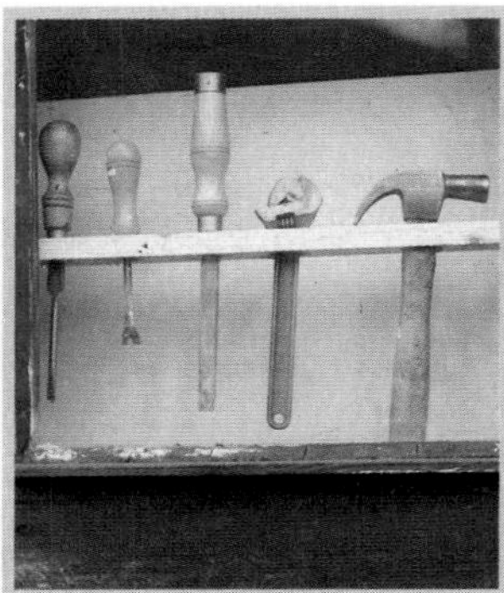

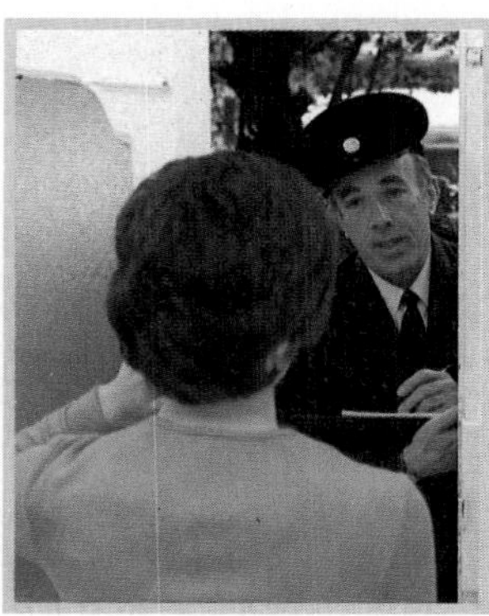

2 Listen to the tape again and complete these sentences.

1 You must be especially careful of ________ ________ ________ ________ ________ ________ ________ .

2 So, ________ ________ , make sure that ________ ________ ________ ________ ________ .

3 For instance, you must remember to ________ ________ ________ .

4 Also, be aware that ________ ________ ________ ________ ________ ________ ________ .

5 And if you're away for several weeks, don't bother ________ ________ ________ ________ ________ .

3 Work in pairs. One of you is a community policeman and the other is a parent who is worried about a number of issues currently causing concern in the neighbourhood:

- young children being abducted by strangers
- road safety, especially for cyclists
- glue sniffing and drugs

Ask for and give advice on these problems.

4 House-breaking is one of the crimes on the increase, especially in cities. Why do you think this is? What other problems do large cities face today?

D

CRIME IN YOUR LOCAL AREA

1 Rank the following criminals according to the seriousness of the crime. Compare your ranking with other students' rankings.

- ☐ cat burglar
- ☐ con-man
- ☐ jay-walker
- ☐ litter bug
- ☐ mugger
- ☐ murderer
- ☐ pick pocket
- ☐ rapist
- ☐ robber
- ☐ thief
- ☐ vandal

2 How important and effective is crime prevention? Why do you think residents of a community are especially equipped to help the police fight crime?

3 Many areas have set up 'Neighbourhood Watch' schemes. Work in small groups. Read the aims of Neighbourhood Watch and decide what practical things you could do to be a good neighbour. Make notes of your suggestions and share them with the rest of the class.

The aims of Neighbourhood Watch

- to reduce local opportunities for crime thereby deterring would-be thieves and vandals;
- to establish a community spirit so that everyone can contribute towards the protection of their property by mutual co-operation and communication;
- to inform the co-ordinator or the police of any suspicious activity.

LEARNING TO LEARN

Tick the following if they are true for you.

In the last few days . . .

1 I've listened to some songs.
2 I've listened to a radio play.
3 I've had a conversation on the telephone.
4 I've overheard a conversation at a bus-stop/in a cafe.
5 I've watched a soap opera on television.
6 I've worked in the language laboratory by myself.
7 I've been in a group (inside or outside the classroom) where people have been speaking English.

Compare your answers with other students', and then consider these questions.

1 What helped you to understand in the situations you ticked?
2 Was it always the same?
3 Did you understand every word?
4 Did it matter to you if you couldn't?

UNIT

8

SPEAK YOUR MIND!

Asking for opinions **Giving opinions** **Agreeing and disagreeing**
Expressing no opinion

Modern life **Issues and causes**

A

STREET INTERVIEWS

1 Listen to the tape. Complete the interviewer's questions, and find and complete the appropriate answers.

1 What _______ _______ _______ _______ modern _______ ?
2 What _______ _______ _______ _______ modern buildings?
3 What _______ _______ _______ _______ _______ ?
4 What _______ _______ _______ _______ pop music?

☐ I _______ them.
They're too _______
and all that glass
and concrete looks
_______ . They're
_______ .

☐ I _______ it.
It's _______ and
_______ , an example
of our colourful times.

☐ Well, _______ _______
_______ it's _______
but perhaps that's
because I'm too old for
all that _______ .
I'm _______ I'm a
bit past it! But
young people need
something of their own.

☐ I haven't really thought
about it so I don't
_______ _______ .
I suppose they're a
_______ _______ .
They're _______ and
more _______
because everything is
in the same place, but
they're _______
_______ for _______
_______ and I _______
all that canned music.
Everything is pre-
packed, too. Me, I think
I _______ the
old-fashioned markets.

2 Work in pairs. Ask and answer the four questions in A1. Give *your* opinions.

3 Find the positive adjectives that correspond to this rather negative list.

awful	ugly
terrible	tasteless
boring	unhealthy
useless	uncomfortable
badly made	expensive

4 Work in small groups and discuss your opinions about some of the aspects of modern life in the list below.

1. Fast/Convenience foods
2. Fashionable clothes, hairstyles, cosmetics
3. Microwave ovens
4. Amusement arcades
5. Video hire shops
6. Modern art and design
7. Grand Prix racing
8. Computers/Word processors
9. Personal stereos
10. Hypermarkets

B

A TELEVISION INTERVIEW

1 Listen to the interview. Write down the three questions and make notes on the answers.

2 Look at these expressions of agreement and disagreement about Nigel Denton's opinions. Which phrases are more formal/polite and which are more informal/impolite/strong? Try saying them.

	Agreement	**Disagreement**
He thinks football hooligans are crazy.	I agree. So do I. I think so too.	I disagree. Does he? I don't. I don't think so.
He doesn't think schools are strict enough these days.	Neither do I. I don't think so either.	Doesn't he? I do. I'm afraid I disagree; I think they're too strict.
In his opinion trial marriages allow people to learn more about each other.	That's very true. Exactly. Yes, indeed. You're quite right.	Nonsense. You're wrong. I can't agree with you there.

3 In groups, discuss *your* reactions to Nigel Denton's opinions.

THE TROUBLE WITH THE WORLD TODAY . . .

1 Being diplomatic

Match the questions with the answers. Why are the answers diplomatic?

THAT'S NOT QUITE TRUE. I THINK THAT MOST PEOPLE CARE A LOT.

YES, BUT WHAT ABOUT THE PEOPLE IN THE THIRD WORLD?

I DON'T COMPLETELY AGREE WITH YOU. IT ALL DEPENDS ON YOUR POINT OF VIEW. SURELY WE SHOULD HELP CRIMINALS?

YES, I AGREE. BUT DON'T YOU THINK IT'S NECESSARY FOR BOTH THE ECONOMY AND PERSONAL FREEDOM?

WOULDN'T YOU SAY THAT EVERYBODY EATS TOO MUCH TODAY?

DON'T YOU THINK THERE'S TOO MUCH TRAFFIC ON THE ROADS? IT SHOULD BE LIMITED.

IT SEEMS TO ME THAT WE SPEND TOO MUCH MONEY ON MAKING PRISONS COMFORTABLE. WHAT DO YOU THINK?

WOULDN'T YOU AGREE THAT PEOPLE DON'T CARE ENOUGH ABOUT OTHERS?

2

Now work in small groups to discuss the issues behind the headlines below.

Doctor defends home births

Toxic plant closed for inquiry after radioactive leak kills one

An affair doesn't mean a divorce!

Duke calls for fresh philosophy on wildlife

'No indoctrination' in school peace studies

Tougher rules on use of pesticides

Terrorist jailed for 25 years

P.M. looks to clean up TV

Now is the hour for Europe's peace people to strike

D I DON'T REALLY KNOW . . .

1 You are at a political rally. There are a lot of pressure groups there who are trying to gain support for their various causes. They are canvassing members of the public to find out exactly what people think, but without much success! Here are some of the answers. What else could you say?

Do you think that boxing should be banned?

I don't really know.

I must admit I've never really thought about it.

I'm afraid I don't have any strong views on the subject.

2 Work in pairs. Practise being equally non-committal and hesitant about the following causes, or any that particularly concern you.

3 Work with a partner to decide on certain political, social and moral issues which *you* feel are important. Write a questionnaire to survey the other students on these questions.

Cause	Agree	Disagree	Don't know

E LEARNING TO LEARN

1 Do you agree or disagree with the following statements?

1 If I make a grammatical mistake, people won't understand what I say.
2 It's worse to make a mistake when you write than when you speak.
3 Small children make mistakes when they're learning their own language, so it seems only natural for people to make mistakes when they're learning a foreign language.
4 I don't see how I can learn if I'm not corrected all the time.
5 Sometimes it's annoying to be corrected when you're in the middle of an interesting conversation.

2 How do you feel when you know you've made a mistake?

1 guilty? **2** angry? **3** upset? **4** irritated? **5** indifferent? **6** . . . ?

3 When you make a mistake, do you expect . . .

1 to be corrected by the teacher?
2 to be corrected by your fellow-students?
3 to correct it yourself (with the help of reference books) once it has been pointed out to you?
4 to receive no correction at all?

Discuss your answers with other students.

UNIT 9

FEELINGS

Expressing feelings Reacting
Gestures Romantic fiction

A DESCRIBING FEELINGS

1 Read this extract from a short story. What kind of story is it? How do the characters in the story feel? How do you know?

Julie frowned. It wasn't like him to be late. Where on earth was he?
John saw her waiting by the bridge. She was tapping her foot and staring miserably into the distance. She didn't notice when he came up behind her, so he tapped her on the shoulder. She almost jumped out of her skin.
"Don't do that!" she shouted. "Where have you been? You're late!" "Oh dear!" he thought, "Now she's in a bad mood." But he smiled. "Sorry, I had to pick this up on the way." He gave her a small box. Her heart missed a beat when she looked inside – it was a __________! "You mean . . .?" she gasped. "Yes," he said, "__________?" She didn't know whether to laugh or cry.

Underline the words in the story which might suggest how the characters feel. What do you think the missing words might be?

2 People show their emotions by their behaviour and by the gestures they make as well as by the words they use and how they say them.

Imagine you were at a party last night. A man called Donald was there and he kept saying or doing the wrong thing. Everyone was having a good time until he spoke to them. When he spoke to them, they behaved in the following ways. Discuss with a partner what each person felt and the sort of thing Donald said to them or told them.

1 Sally looked at Donald and yawned.
2 Dipak first scratched his head and then shook it.
3 Janet slapped his face and walked away.
4 Jill went red in the face.
5 Stan gaped and raised his eyebrows.
6 Susan went as white as a ghost and jumped on a chair.
7 Dina sighed and sat in the corner with her head in her hands.
8 Margaret started wringing her hands.
9 Lucy read Donald's note, then nodded and blew him a kiss.
10 Walter, Pamela's fiancé, shook his fist and stamped out of the room.
11 Alison burst into tears.
12 The dog started jumping up and down, barking and wagging its tail.

3 What other gestures can you think of? What do they mean? What feelings do they show?

In groups, mime some feelings using gestures. The other students must guess what feeling you have expressed.

B

BEING SYMPATHETIC

1 Listen to these two conversations. How do the people feel, and why?

Conversation 1
Dick feels ____________ because ____________.
Sam feels ____________ because ____________.

Conversation 2
Dick feels ____________ because ____________.
Sam feels ____________ because ____________.

2 **Language study**

Sam says: 'How exciting!'
What is exciting? Who is excited?

Sam says: 'How disappointing?'
What is disappointing? Who is disappointed?

Many of the words which describe feelings work in the same way as *excited/exciting* and *disappointing/disappointed*. Can you think of any? Put them in a table.

He's excited about the trip. He's disappointed about it.	The trip is exciting. It's disappointing.

3 What if . . . ?

Sam says: 'I'd be thrilled!'
What would he be thrilled about? Is he thrilled now?

Work in pairs or small groups. Discuss how you would feel in these situations.

How would you feel if . . .

1 you were going to China for six months?
2 you were alone in a dark forest at night?
3 you were climbing Mount Everest?
4 you were at the top of Mount Everest?
5 you were taking your driving test?
6 you were in a plane when it ran out of fuel?
7 you couldn't find your way home?
8 you were at an interview for a job?

4

Think of an important situation in your life. Think of how you felt and why. Go over the situation in your mind and re-live it.

Work in small groups. Tell the people in your group what happened to you and how you felt.

C EXPRESSING YOUR FEELINGS

1

Listen to the conversations and consider these questions:

1 Who are the people and what is the relationship between them?
2 What situation are they in?
3 What feelings are they expressing?

2

Listen to the first conversation again. What other ways are there of introducing and reacting to surprising news? Make a list.

Introducing the news	Reacting to the news
You'll never guess what happened?	She hasn't, has she?
Did you know that . . . ?	Never!
. . .	. . .

3

Work in pairs. You are A or B. Read your news headlines and write notes about the stories. Tell your partner the surprising news.

Student A

PRINCESS TO MARRY BANK CLERK
MAN FINDS GOLD IN GARDEN
Woman has Sextuplets
Snow in the Sahara
MARTIANS VISITING EARTH
MAN BITES DOG

Student B

LION ESCAPES FROM ZOO
LOCH NESS MONSTER TO HAVE BABY
Beer cheaper
CAT CAN TALK
Girl Climbs Everest Alone
Girl to Cycle round World

Think of more surprising 'local' news – fact or fiction – to tell your partner.

4 Listen to Conversation 5 again. In situations like these you will have to be very polite, especially if you want to ask rather personal questions or say something which the other person may not like. Think of some more ways of opening such a conversation and replying.

Opening	Positive reply	Negative Reply
Excuse me, I hope you don't mind me asking but . . . I'm sorry to bother you, but . . .	No, not at all. That's quite all right.	I'm sorry, I'm rather busy. Well, actually, I *am* in the middle of something.

5 Work with a partner. You are on a train and have never met before. Use your lists in C4 to help you make conversations for the situations below.

Student A	Student B
1 You are sitting opposite Student B who looks very upset. You wonder why. You are very sympathetic.	You're very upset. Your fiancée has left you and you feel lonely. You wish you could talk to someone. It might help.
2 You're very worried. You're a student and your exams begin tomorrow, so you must study. You don't really want to talk to anyone!	You're 17 and have just left home for the first time to travel round England. You love talking to people. The person opposite looks interesting but seems to be worried. Ask if he/she is all right.

D FRIEND OR FOE?

1 When you want to complain about something or be angry with someone, your language will depend on whether you are talking to a stranger or a friend.

Complaining to a stranger **Reacting to a complaint**

Complaining to a friend **Reacting to a complaint**

What else could you say?

2 Practise in pairs.

Student A	Student B
1 Your neighbour's dog keeps coming in your garden. It digs up all your most beautiful flowers. Talk to him/her about it. He/she really should control the dog. If it happens again, you'll call the police!	Your neighbour complains about everything, and loses his/her temper very quickly. Yesterday your beautiful Great Dane went into his/her garden for a few minutes. It's the first time, and you couldn't stop it.
2 You are 15. All of your friends can do anything they want to, but your parents are always angry with you. You think they are unfair. Last night you went to a party. You had your hair done and bought some new clothes for it. You missed the last bus home!	Your son/daughter is 15, and never listens to you. This time he/she has gone too far – bright red hair! Those terrible clothes! And he/she stayed out all night! You are angry. You think that his/her friends are not very nice. You want him/her to stay away from them.

3 Degrees of politeness

How you express your feelings depends, of course, on who you are speaking to. What would you say in these situations to . . .

– a friend?
– a complete stranger?
– a policeman?

1 This car is always parked across your driveway so that you can't get in or out of your house. You've had enough.
2 You are on the beach when you see an enormous shark.
3 You see a big black bag in the railway station which doesn't seem to belong to anyone. You think it's a bomb.
4 You're curious. The person next to you seems to be wearing pyjamas.

E

THEMES

Work in small groups. Look at the following themes and discuss . . .

1 the situations you associate with each theme
2 the feelings you associate with each theme
3 the words and phrases which best describe the feelings

Your group task is to produce a short story or a short poem which expresses or arouses the feeling of one theme.

F

LEARNING TO LEARN

1 Rank the following statements according to the way you like working most.

I enjoy . . .

- ☐ working on a new exercise with the person sitting next to me
- ☐ sharing information or discussing with a small group of students
- ☐ listening to the teacher explain something
- ☐ walking round the room to find information or complete a task
- ☐ using things not 'normally' associated with the classroom, e.g. music
- ☐ copying from the blackboard
- ☐ doing work which takes me outside the classroom
- ☐ roleplays, because you practise different sorts of language

Discuss your answers in groups and consider the question: What were your main objections to the statement(s) you ranked lowest?

2 Do you agree or disagree?

1 I don't like roleplays because I can't see the point of pretending to be someone else.
2 Doing roleplays helps me to understand other people's point of view.
3 I like working in pairs because I get a chance to speak.
4 I don't like working with other students because I'll learn their mistakes.
5 I don't see how our teacher can hear what we're all saying when we are doing pairwork.
6 When we work in groups, X does all the talking and I never get a chance.

REVIEW UNIT 3

PART 1 LANGUAGE REVIEW

Asking for and giving advice **Giving opinions**

The British education system **The Open University**

A

PATHWAYS

1 Study the chart below and listen to Gary, Jeff, Lara and Tor talking about the schools and colleges they attend. What kind of school or college do they go to?

1 Gary goes to .....
2 Jeff goes to .....
3 Lara goes to .....
4 Tor goes to .....

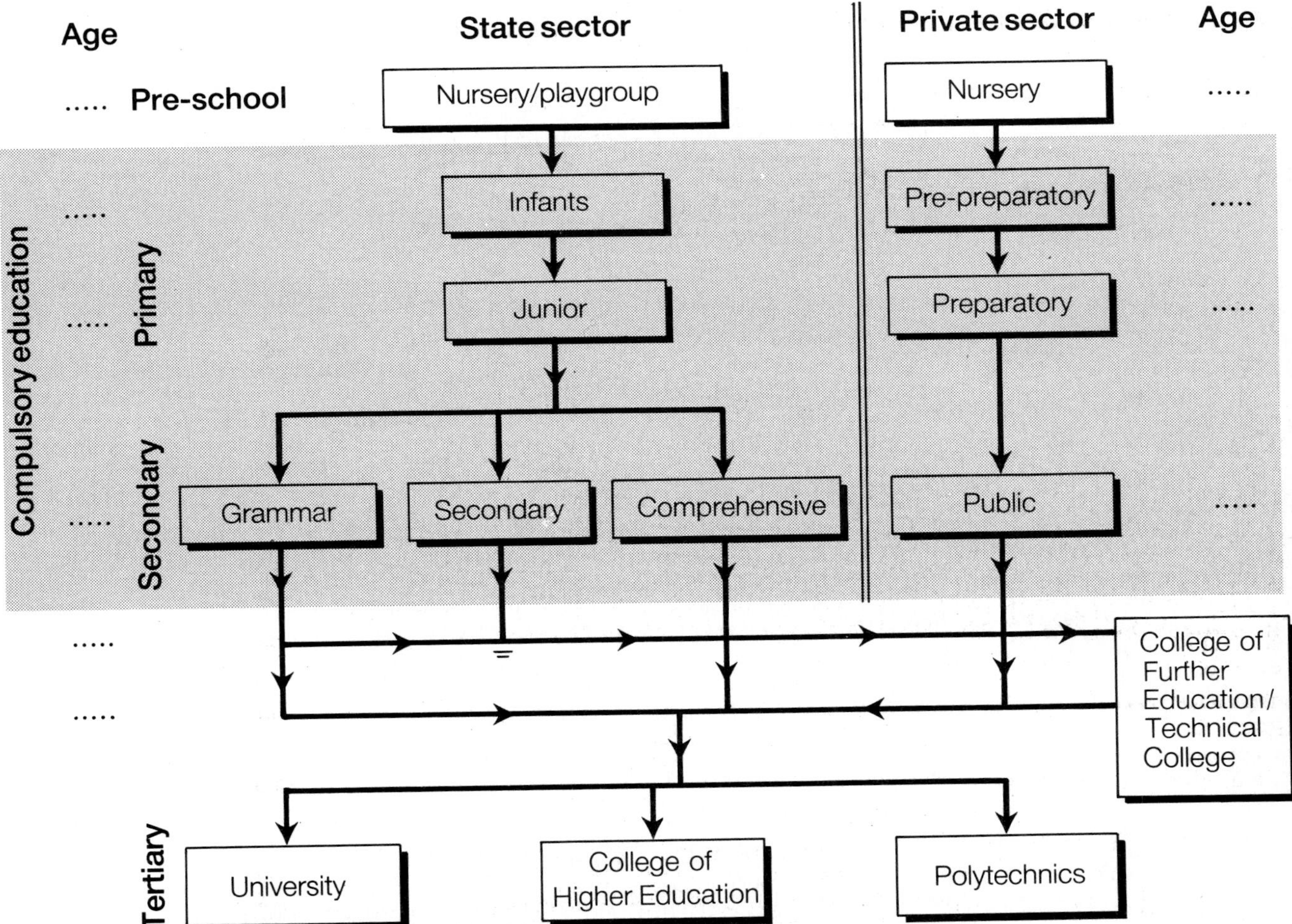

2 On the chart above, fill in the ages at which you think people attend these educational institutions. Compare the system with the educational system in your own country. Are the systems the same? How do they differ?

B

THE OPEN UNIVERSITY

1 What do you know about the Open University in Britain? How does it fit into the general educational system in Britain? Is there an equivalent in your country?

2 Viv's friend is thinking of taking an Open University course. She/he asks advice from Viv. Read the extracts from Viv's letter. What advice does she give? Does she think an Open University course is a good thing?

"... You asked me about doing an Open University course, if I thought it would be a good idea for you.

Well, the first thing you have to ask yourself is 'Do I want to do it?' - you need to be highly motivated as it means studying alone. If I were you, I'd consider the other alternatives - colleges, polytechnics or universities - where you can get a degree on a full-time course. With the Open University, if you do one credit a year (which most people find enough) it takes you six years for an ordinary degree and eight for an honours degree. I don't know whether you have any Further Education qualifications (i.e. above A-levels) but if you have, sometimes the Open University will give you some credits for those.

It seems to me, though, that it could be a good idea for you, with the children and house and everything. Basically, it's a question of whether you can find a regular slot for studying; they reckon 12-14 hours a week is the minimum, though you'll need more than that on a full-credit course when an assignment is due. You need to get yourself organized for time and space (a corner to work in) and you have to be very disciplined.

How does Dave feel about it? It's very important that you get his support. Perhaps he'd like to do a course too!

The course material is very good. There are units to read and a few set books. Some courses have TV or radio programmes too, which go out at unearthly hours of the day or night; so it's handy if you've got a video and a radio cassette you can pre-set to record the programmes for you - getting up at 5.30 a.m. I've found impossible!

In your first year, or foundation course, there are regular tutorials, which are a great help. They drop to four or five tutorials a year later. Then there's the summer school. All foundation courses and some others have a summer school. These are a week of intensive study - and fun! - at a university or college. They are an integral part of the course, so you'd have to be able to organize Dave or your mother to look after the kids.

On a full-credit course, there are about seven or eight assignments a year (roughly one a month) and an exam at the end. I'm trying to revise for that now - and instead I'm writing to you! That's what I mean about being disciplined!

If I were you, I'd do a foundation course and see how you get on. If you don't like the method of study (you might find it a bit solitary for example), it would always be useful for getting you on a full-time course somewhere else later.

Anyway, that's my advice! Hope you had a good time at the wedding last week. Fancy them finally taking the plunge! I bet it was a surprise to Janet ..."

3 Divide into two groups. Group A is Viv, Group B is Viv's friend. Read the instructions for your group and between you work out what you are going to say.

Group A: Viv

You have been doing an Open University course for about three years now. Now it is your turn to give advice! With all the other commitments in your life (decide what these are), you've found it hard work, working on your own and having to get assignments in on time. You're not sure you would have done it if you had known the commitment it involved. Perhaps a full-time university or polytechnic course would be better. Think about the problem. Be prepared to advise your friend when he/she rings up.

Group B: Viv's friend

You have asked your friend Viv for some advice on doing an Open University course. She has been doing one for about three years. She wrote and told you all the difficulties, but before you enrol, you want to discuss it with her again. You have discussed the situation with your husband/wife (decide what his/her opinion is).

Now divide into pairs, one from Group A and one from Group B, and have the telephone conversation.

C

WHAT SHOULD I DO?

1 Listen once to Jeff, Gary, Lara and Tor giving advice. What do Lara and Tor say is the most important thing to do at secondary school and at technical college?

Listen again. What does Jeff advise children not to do at primary school? Does Gary agree with him? What do Lara and Tor say about discipline?

2 What advice would you give someone who asked you about going to study in another country? Would you recommend it, or is it better to carry on studying in your own country?

D

OPINIONS ABOUT SCHOOL

1 Listen to Lara, Tor, Gary and Jeff again. Who is enthusiastic about school? Who is not? Why do you think they like or dislike school or college?

2 Who do you think said which of these statements: Gary, Jeff, Tor or Lara?

1 I think school should start at four years old so you can make friends earlier.
2 I don't think children should be made to do subjects they don't like.
3 In my opinion everyone should have a year off school at 16.
4 I don't think school should be compulsory.

E FEELINGS ABOUT SCHOOL

1 Did you like school? Which words describe your schooldays? Write down as many other words as you can think of to describe how you felt about school.

OK **interesting** **boring** **all right, I suppose** **enjoyable** **best time of my life**

2 In groups, use the words from E1 to help you write a poem about school. Begin each line with these letters:

S . . .
C . . .
H . . .
O . . .
O . . .
L . . .

Here's a poem that Tor and his friends wrote:

Stringing along corridors
Cold classrooms
Hot, sticky hands
'Orrible dinners
Outward confidence, inward fears
Lost, lazy days

F LEARNING TO LEARN

Below is a list of the language items you have studied in Units 7–9; the numbers in brackets refer to the units. Grade yourself according to how well you think you can now do these things.

√√√ very well
√√ quite well
√ need more practice

Can you . . .

ask for advice (7)?
give advice (7)?
ask for an opinion (8)?
give an opinion (8)?
express no opinion (8)?
agree and disagree (8)?
ask about and express feelings (9)?
open a conversation with a stranger (9)?
introduce and react to surprising news (9)?
complain politely and angrily (9)?

PART 2 SIMULATION

A DEVELOPED AND DEVELOPING COUNTRIES

1 Work in groups of three to complete as much as you can of this table. Then compare your answers with other groups.

Country	Continent	Developed?	Income per head
Brazil			
Australia			
Tanzania			
Kuwait			
Thailand			
Japan			

2 True (T) or false (F)? Work in groups of three, then compare your answers with the other groups.

1 Europe is more civilized than other continents.
2 There is only one cause of poverty.
3 The Western idea of development is the best idea of development.
4 Developing countries are all very similar.
5 People in developing countries have only physical needs.
6 People in developing countries lead happy, carefee lives.
7 Population is man's greatest problem.
8 Technology will provide all the answers to the Third World's problems.
9 Women must be involved in the development process.
10 Rich countries should send their food surpluses to poor countries.

3 In small groups decide what you think are the main industrial, economic, political and social priorities in developed countries and contrast them with those in developing countries. Some examples have been given.

Priorities	Developed countries	Developing countries
Industrial	– reduce unemployment	– provide industrial base
Economic	– reduce inflation	– infrastructure
Political	– doctrine *v.* pragmatism	– democracy
Social	– use of leisure	– housing
Other		

B

KELAPIA – PROFILE OF A DEVELOPING COUNTRY

1 Study the map of Kelapia. What resources does it possess?

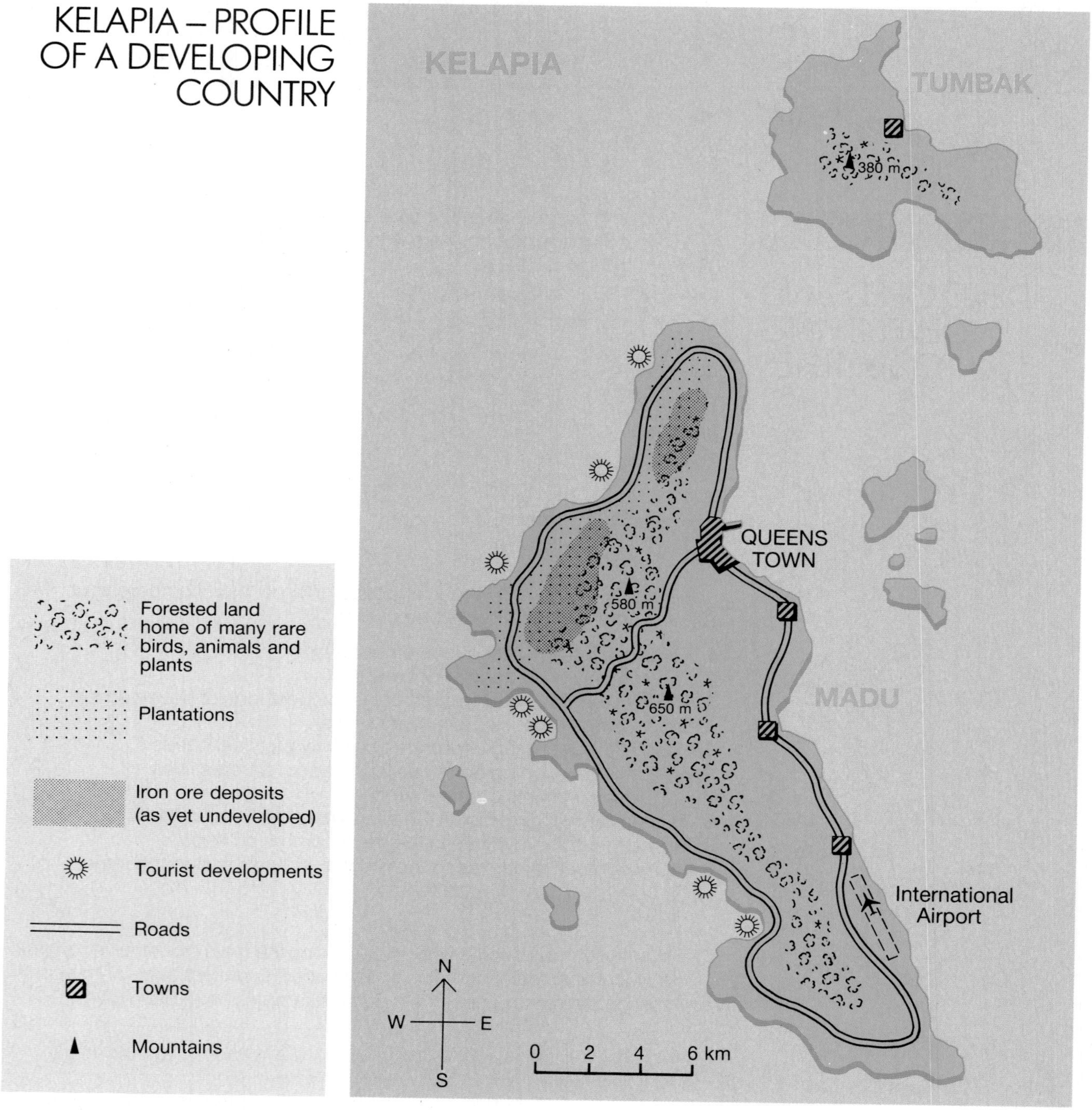

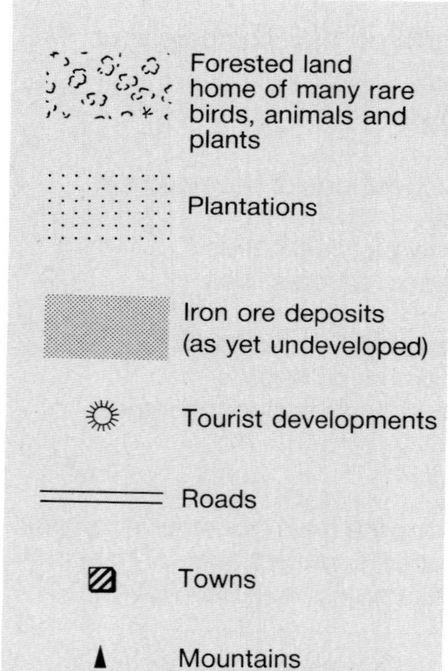

2 Work in groups of five. Each person in the group should read one of the pieces on Kelapia on the next page and then share the information to answer these five questions.

1 Where is Kelapia located?
2 What happened within a year of Kelapia gaining independence?
3 Which ethnic groups live on Kelapia?
4 What is the predominant religion of the country?
5 What was the traditional pattern of agriculture?

GEOGRAPHY

Kelapia is a small, island republic located roughly 900 miles off the coast of Africa in the Indian Ocean. It consists of two main islands, Madu and Tumbak and over 100 scattered islets, most of which are uninhabited. The archipelago lies totally within the tropics and has a monsoon climate. The total land area is 285 square kilometres, Madu (196 sq.km.), Tumbak 53 sq.km.). The main island, home of over 90% of the population, has many fine beaches, small stretches of coastal lowland used for agriculture and a mountainous and densely forested central ridge. There is plenty of fresh water on Madu though water becomes scarce on Tumbak during the dry season and there is very little ground water on any of the remaining islands.

HISTORY

Kelapia was first colonized by the French in the 18th century and ceded to the British in 1814. Plantations were established and labourers brought in from mainland African territories and the Indian subcontinent. Kelapia was granted its independence from Britain in 1979. Free elections were held and a progressive pro-western government was returned. However, within a year a military coup took place, reflecting deep-seated instability within the political system. The new government claims to be socialist and has the support of the Soviet Union, though it has yet to implement any far-reaching policy changes due to the strong colonial economic legacy.

ETHNIC COMPOSITION

The islanders are ethnically very mixed. The indigenous inhabitants, known as Kelawi, have intermarried to a certain extent but still preserve a distinct culture and ethnic identity. Later arrivals to the islands include a large number of East Africans and a smaller number of Indians from the Bombay area. Finally there is a small residual population of British and other European settlers.

Population by Ethnic Composition (%)

Kelawi	35%
African	40%
Indian	15%
Mixed	8%
Others	2%

RELIGION

Kelapia recognizes the right of the individual to practise any religion, as long as it does not conflict with the constitution and national interests. The majority of the Kelawi and Africans were missionized during the colonial period though the Indians have on the whole retained Hinduism as their faith. Both Kelawi and Africans mix Christianity and animism in their practices.

Population by Religion (%)

Protestant	65%
Catholic	23%
Hindu	10%
Muslim	2%

ECONOMY

The traditional base of the economy was, for over a century, plantation agriculture, relying on the export of copra and coconut products, cinnamon and vanilla. However, during the early 1960s the productivity of the coconut plantations declined due to the age of many of the palms and poor management of the estates, while the world market price of vanilla slumped drastically. Even though the value of cinnamon rose sharply during the same period, the government was forced to consider alternative sources of revenue.

3 As the traditional base of the Kelapian economy had disappeared, the government was forced to consider alternative sources of revenue. The solution they adopted was the development of tourism and in 1971 an international airport was opened, effectively ending hundreds of years of cultural isolation for Kelapia.

1 Why do you think that Kelapia became a popular holiday destination?
2 What effects would the tourist boom have on the people of Kelapia? In particular consider the effect on the following group of people who all live in one of the small fishing villages of the North which the government decides to develop.

a fisherman
the mayor of the village
a child of school age
an unemployed teenager
a woodcarver
the wife of a fisherman
a plantation worker
the landowner of a coconut plantation
a trader in the local market

The statistics in these tables may help you.

Tourist Arrivals

Year	Total Arrivals	Average no. of Tourists on any one day
1967	306	12
1969	350	16
1971	3,611	86
1973	19,484	600
1975	37,321	1,382
1977	75,851	2,011
1979	105,664	2,981
1981	56,409	1,648

Employment Outside of Agriculture and Fishing

Sector	1970	1972	1976	1980
Construction	1,820	4,960	5,083	3,650
Restaurants	650	730	2,108	1,972
Manufacturing	390	540	668	703
Hotels	204	826	1,428	1,635
Transport	1,062	943	1,409	1,448
Administration	1,062	1,128	1,382	2,199
Business	311	344	429	563
Recreation	48	106	304	265
Other services	3,198	4,227	4,929	5,085

Reported Cases of Selected Crimes

Crime	1961	1971	1981
Theft	488	724	1596
Assault	34	280	853
Disorderly Conduct	180	630	1,198
Drug Abuse	—	62	159

C

THE FUTURE OF KELAPIA

The tourist bubble burst in 1980, following a coup and fears concerning security on the islands. At the same time the world economic recession was beginning to take effect and markets began to shrink. Since 1980 tourist arrivals have been steadily falling and once again the government is facing a crisis as the economy is now heavily reliant on tourists.

The government decides to set up working parties to plan the future development of the economy. Work in small 'working parties' and discuss your ideas with reference to the map and the information you now have on Kelapia. Compare your proposals with the other working parties in a joint council meeting.

In addition, you should also discuss the following points, remembering that you don't have to accept any of these alternatives.

1 Russia wants to send engineers to develop the iron ore. They also propose to train Kelapian mineworkers to eventually run the mines themselves. In return they want to extend the docks so that they have somewhere to lay up ships based in the Indian Ocean.

2 The Food and Agricultural Organization is willing to provide some money to explore the possibility of different forms of agriculture. They think more use could be made of the forest.

3 France is prepared to give aid to develop tourism but (under pressure from NATO) only if the Russians are kept out.

4 Conservation Societies are very agitated about the increasing invasion of the forest area, both by farmers and by tourists. There are some forms of wild life there which are found nowhere else in the world and they fear that any disturbance of the forest area could cause some species to be lost forever.

SUPPOSING

Expressing certainty and uncertainty **Speculating about the future**

Science fiction

A

POSSIBILITIES

1 Dominique, the French assistante at the Technical College in Torquay, would like to be able to stay in England for the summer, but she needs a job. Listen and answer the questions.

1 What are the five job possibilities Dominique mentions?
2 What does she think her parents will worry about?
3 How long will she stay if she finds a job which lasts longer than two months?
4 How many of the following expressions does she use to express her uncertainty about the summer?

Well, if that happens,	I'll I think I'll I expect I'll I suppose I'll	go back to France.

2 Write these phrases in appropriate columns.

Maybe I'll stay in England.
I definitely won't stay . . .
I'll probably stay . . .
I suppose I could stay . . .
I think I'll stay . . .
I'll stay in England.
I doubt if I'll stay . . .
I expect I'll stay . . .
I'm sure I won't stay . . .
I might possibly stay . . .
I probably won't stay . . .
I don't think I'll stay . . .

certainty	possibility	perhaps	uncertainty	definitely not

3 It's clear that Dominique's family will discuss her summer plans with her over the telephone. Divide into two groups. One group is Dominique's parents, the other group is Dominique herself. In groups discuss what you are going to say. Then find a partner from another group and act out the phone-call.

4 Have you any decisions to make about your future? Discuss them with a partner.

B SPECULATION

1 What would you do if you had £50,000? Make notes, then in groups tell each other your answers. You can use the language in A2 again, but you'll need to make some changes. What are they?

2 How did you answer B1? Did you say you would lead much the same life, only a little more luxuriously? Then, according to some psychologists, you are already leading the right sort of life for you. On the other hand, if your answer was very different from your present lifestyle, then maybe you are not doing the right thing for you.

This is what the writer and poet D. H. Lawrence said:

> *When I wish I was rich, then I know I am ill.*
> *Because, to tell the truth, I have enough as I am.*
> *So when I catch myself thinking: Ah, if I was rich . . .*
> *I say to myself: Hello! I'm not well. My vitality is low.*

In groups, discuss your answers to B1 again in the light of the above.

3 In pairs or small groups, look at the following unlikely situations and say what you would do and how you would feel . . .

- if your company was being moved 500 kms. away
- if you inherited a house in need of repair
- if a stray dog 'adopted' you
- if a number of relatives decided to visit you at the same time
- if a stranger offered to buy your car on the spot, for cash

C IMAGINATION

1 Sometimes we like to speculate about very unlikely situations. In small groups, discuss some of the following ideas. Let your imaginations go!

'I wonder what it'd be like if they built cities under the sea.'

'I wonder what it'd be like to be very famous.'

'Supposing we could become invisible at will!'

'Supposing we could go to sleep and wake up in a hundred years' time.'

'I think it'd be wonderful to be a real live superman – to be able to fly!'

'I wonder . . .'

'Supposing . . .'

2 What would you do?

In groups of three, read the first extract of the story below.
Decide what you would do. Then go to the next part of the story you have chosen. Continue in the same way until you reach the final part of the story.

A Story Without End?

1 You wake up one day and find you are in a strange room. You look out of the window and see a strange garden. What would you do?

- call out? (Go to Part 3)
- try to get out of the room? (Go to Part 11)
- stay where you are? (Go to Part 4)

2 The door opens slowly. Through a crack in the cupboard you can just see the outline of some creature. It is dressed very strangely. The creature stops when it sees the bed empty. Would you . . .

- come out of the cupboard? (11)
- stay where you are? (8)
- creep up on the creature and hit it on the head? (9)

3 At first no one responds to your call. Then you hear a strange shuffling sound. A deep voice says something you do not understand. Would you . . .

- stay where you are? (4)
- ask whoever it is to come in? (7)
- hide in a cupboard? (2)

4 You try to go back to sleep but you can't. Outside the window is a strange noise. Would you . . .

- rush to the window and wave? (12)
- try to see without being seen? (15)
- call out? (3)

5 The hat is made of a strange substance you've never seen before. As you pick it up, it crackles. Would you . . .

- throw it out of the window? (4)
- put it down? (13)
- go after the creature and give it back? (11)

6 Outside the corridor is empty. No one anywhere. Would you . . .

- stay in the room? (4)
- go along the corridor? (14)

7 The door opens and a strange creature comes in. Would you . . .

- stare at the creature? (8)
- rush to make it go out of the room? (9)

8 You can scarcely breathe, but you see the creature is all dressed in green with a strange hat on its head. You move and it rushes out of the room. As it goes, it drops the green hat. Would you . . .

- go back to bed? (10)
- follow the creature out of the door? (11)
- pick up the hat? (5)

9 As you hit it on the head, it lets out a strange groan, staggers slightly and then rushes out of the room. As it goes, its funny green hat falls to the ground. Would you . . .

- pick it up? (5)
- rush out after it? (11)
- give a sigh of relief that it's gone? (10)

10 You wake up in your own room and in your own bed. It had all been a dream! Or had it? On the floor by the bed is a green hat that you've never seen before. Whose could it be? Then you hear strange noises outside. What could they be? What would you do?

11 You creep quietly to the door and try the handle, but it won't move! Would you . . .

- call out? (3)
- go back to bed? (4)
- try to break the door down? (6)

12 You look in horror! On the lawn outside are about a dozen strange creatures all dressed in green. Would you . . .

- rush out of the door? (6)
- try to hide in the cupboard? (2)

13 You drop it. Maybe it's a weapon of some sort. The green cap makes a strange sound as it drops. Would you . . .

- leave it there? (4)
- call out? (3)
- wait to see if the creature returns for it? (11)

14 At the end of the corridor is another door. This one is also locked. You can't undo it, no matter how hard you try. So you go back to your room and try to sleep.

(Go to Part 4)

15 A strange aircraft of some sort lands on the lawn outside.

(Go to Part 12)

SCIENCE FICTION

1 Read the passage below and name some science fiction authors.

Science fiction is a form of literature that began to emerge about the beginning of this century. It speculates about the future, asking the question 'What if . . . ?'

What if the world ended in twenty years time?
What if people from another planet invaded the earth?

Some stories are just good adventure stories, but many science fiction writers try to make people aware of the implications of present-day scientific developments.

Jules Verne predicted air travel and submarines. H. G. Wells wrote about the invasion of the earth by Martians. Aldous Huxley in *Brave New World* wrote about the implications of genetic engineering and Ursula Le Guin uses science fiction to talk about the role of women.

Science fiction has produced a number of excellent short stories particularly since the advent of popular magazines in the 1930s. These are a good way to begin reading science fiction.

2 Read the following extract from a short story called *The First Men* by Howard Fast. A young couple Mark and Jean, find forty potentially clever children from all over the world and with forty committed adults bring them up on a reservation in California, far away from the influence of the ordinary world. Free from the stresses of society, the children develop all their skills.

Extract A

In a letter to her brother Harry, Jean explains what happens. What new discovery do the children make that is described here?

It wasn't easy, Harry. We worked and worried to give these children love and teaching. And wonderful things happened. How can I tell you about an American Indian boy who was five years old and who wrote beautiful music? Or the two children, one Italian, one African, who at six years old made a machine to find the speed of light? We, the adults, sat quietly and listened to them explaining their machines to us.

They're not like the clever but unhappy children with parents who say, 'Why can't we have normal children?' Ours *are* normal children, strong, happy, laughing – perhaps the first normal children in the world.

One lovely cool day, Mark and I were walking and we saw some children sitting on the ground. Five of them sat in a ring, with another in the middle. Their heads were together and they were laughing quietly. The other children sat about ten feet away, watching carefully.

When we came nearer, the children outside the ring put their fingers to their mouths to tell us to be quiet. So we stood and watched. About ten minutes later, the little girl in the middle of the ring jumped to her feet shouting, 'I heard you! I heard you!'

Then all the children ran to her and danced around her.

'Aren't we clever?' they asked.

'Yes,' we said. 'Very clever.' But we didn't get too excited; we wanted them to think that it was normal.

Mark told the other teachers about it last night. Dr Goldbaum said, 'Jean, you always said that much of the mind is closed. I think these children have opened it. I think they're learning to listen to thoughts.'

'That can't be true,' said one of the teachers.

'Yes, it can,' said Mark. 'Perhaps it's something which a person must learn when he's very young, or not at all. And don't forget, there's never been an environment like this. Perhaps the environment has helped our children to learn it.'

Do you think it's possible to communicate without speaking? Give examples that you have read or know about.

Extract B

When they are fifteen, the government want to come and inspect the children, but Michael, one of the children, urges Jean to go to Washington and persuade them not to come just yet. Here he explains why.

> 'Then this is what we've decided,' Michael said. 'You, Jean, must go to Washington with Mark and get more time. Then we must bring more children into the reservation and teach them here.'
>
> 'But why must you bring them here?' Mark asked. 'You can go into their minds and share your thoughts with them.'
>
> 'But *they* can't go into *our* minds,' Michael said. 'And they'll be in danger. What will the people in the world outside do to children like that? No, we must bring more children here, hundreds more. Then there must be other reservations like this one. It'll take a long time – the world is very big and there are a lot of children. And we must work carefully or the other people will kill us.'

Why are the children a danger to the outside world? Do you agree?

What do you think happens to the reservation? In groups, write your own ending to the story.

3 Many people today are worried about the implications of current development in science and technology. Look at the list below, and add two worries of your own. Then rank the items from 1 to 10 according to which worries you most (1) and which worries you least (10).

- ☐ test-tube babies
- ☐ chemical warfare
- ☐ tablets to cure everything
- ☐ predicting the sex of babies
- ☐ 'Star Wars'
- ☐ extending human life expectancy
- ☐ 'Big is Best' in the development of cities
- ☐ Government 'interference' in family size
- ☐ . . .
- ☐ . . .

Discuss your answers with the rest of the class.

E

LEARNING TO LEARN

Discuss these statements with other students and compare your opinions.

1. It's not my fault if I don't learn – it's my teacher's.
2. I really enjoy my English classes.
3. I often ask another student to help me if my teacher is busy helping someone else.
4. If I can't follow something, I ask questions.
5. If my teacher asks me to do something different in a lesson, I understand that she/he has a good reason and that it will help me improve my English.

UNIT 11 WHAT ON EARTH. . .?

Deducing Speculating

Museum pieces Mysteries: The Bermuda Triangle

A

WHO OR WHAT CAN IT BE?

1 One of these people is waiting to see you outside.

Robert

John

Sue

Dave

Anna

Pauline

Clues

	Impossible	**Possible**	**Sure**
1 It isn't a man.	It *can't be* John, Dave or Robert	It *could/might/may be* Anna, Sue or Pauline.	
2 She hasn't got long hair.	It *can't be* Anna.	It *could be* Sue or Pauline.	
3 She wears glasses.	It *can't be* Sue.		It *must be* Pauline.

2 Look at the pictures below and discuss what you think they could be. If you can, come to a group decision about what they must be.

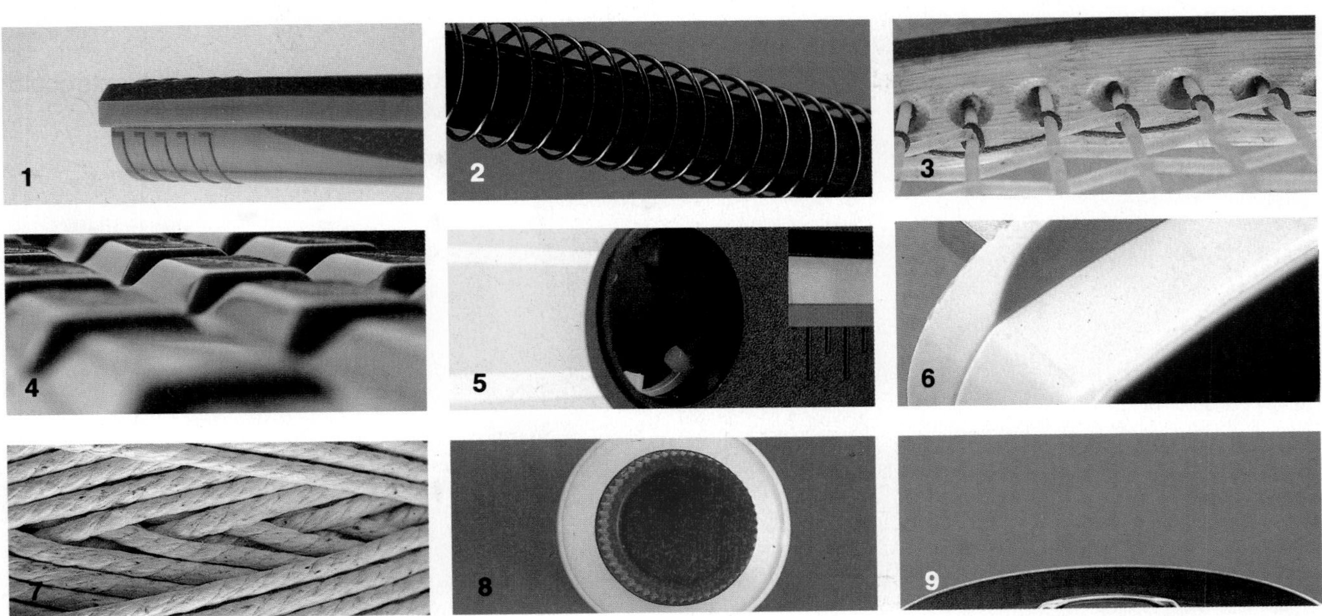

B

WHO OR WHAT CAN IT HAVE BEEN?

1 Pauline found something in the street a few weeks ago and took it to the police. It was one of these things:

a puppy, a gold watch, a pair of woollen gloves, a diamond necklace, an umbrella

Work out what it was.

Clues

	Impossible	**Possible**	**Sure**
1 It wasn't alive, so . . .	It *can't have been* the puppy.	It *could have been* the umbrella.	
2 It was very valuable, so . . .	It *couldn't have been* the gloves.	It *might have been* the watch.	
3 It's worn round the neck, so . . .	It *can't have been* the watch.		It *must have been* the necklace.

2 It was Dave's daughter Carolyn's birthday last week but she didn't receive a card from her boyfriend. Dave told her he must have forgotten. Carolyn suspects he might have found a new girlfriend.

Draw more conclusions for the following situations.

1 My neighbours were in hospital for six months.
2 I stayed awake last night reading a book.
3 I used to live next door to a couple who argued all the time.
4 A fourteen-year-old girl ran away from home.
5 A colleague of mine left the office at lunchtime and didn't come back.
6 Aunt Jane didn't arrive on the 7.40 train as she said she would.

C

MUSEUM PIECES

1 Listen to the recording. What are the old lady and Hank looking at?

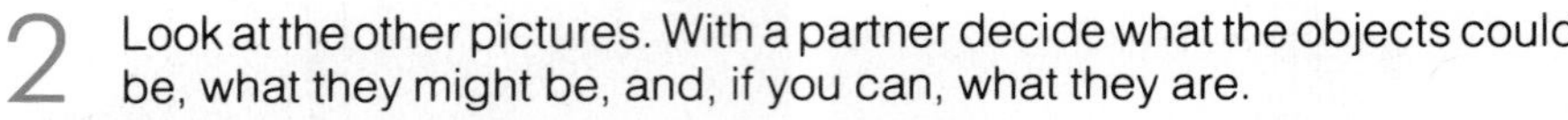

2 Look at the other pictures. With a partner decide what the objects could be, what they might be, and, if you can, what they are.

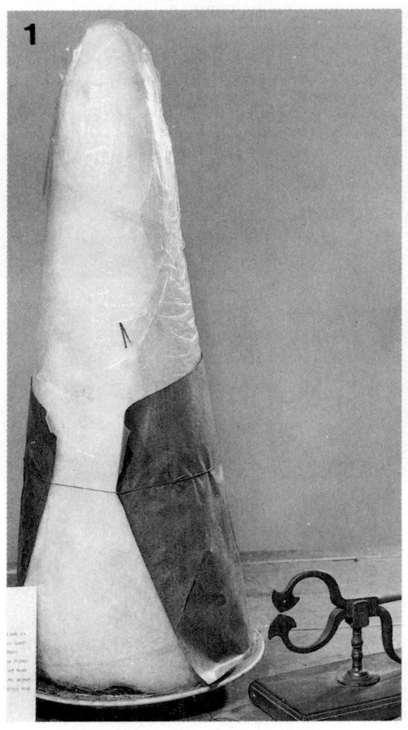

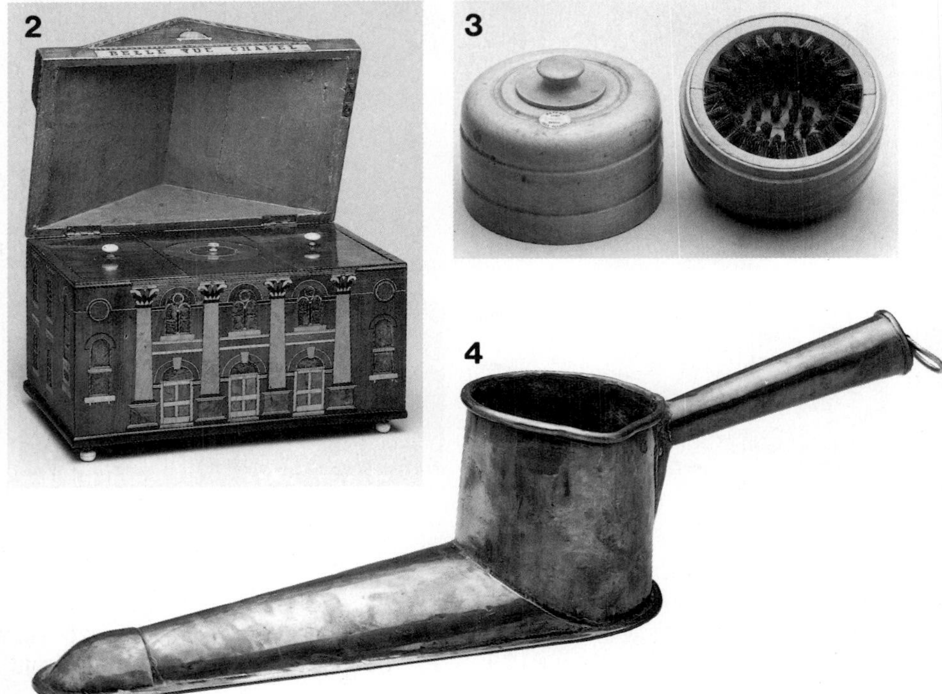

D

THE BERMUDA TRIANGLE

In the area known as the Bermuda Triangle, some of the world's greatest unsolved mysteries have occurred. More than 100 boats and planes have literally disappeared into thin air, mostly since 1945. Over 1000 people have been lost without a single body being recovered; nor has there been a trace of any wreckage from the ships or planes.

Several theories have been put forward to account for this phenomenon which range from a natural, but as yet unexplained, electromagnetic force, to mysterious beings from outer space doing research on mankind.

1 Divide into three groups. Each group read one of the accounts on the next page of mysteries of the Bermuda Triangle, and answer the questions. Discuss what might have happened and what couldn't have happened.

2 Re-form into groups of three people (one person from each original group) and tell each other your stories and theories.

3 Discuss any other mysteries in the world that you have heard of, e.g. Atlantis, the Ley-lines of Peru and elsewhere, the Yeti, etc.

Mystery 1

We know that from 1945 to 1965 fifteen aeroplanes from major airlines disappeared in the area as well as a high number of military and private aeroplanes. The following story is a typical example.

Caroline Cascio, piloting a light aircraft, together with a passenger disappeared on June 7 1964 while on a flight from Nassau to Grand Turk Island in the Bahamas. When she got to the point where, according to her calculations, she should have been arriving at her destination, she called up on the radio and said in a distressed voice that she was flying over unidentifiable islands, adding paradoxically, 'There's nothing under me!' Later she cried, 'How can we get out of here?'

Curiously, observers from Grand Turk Island had noticed a small aeroplane flying over the island for about half an hour before disappearing. Those words were the last trace of her or her aeroplane. Extensive searches were made, but nothing was found.

True or false?

1 Fifteen planes disappeared in twenty years.
2 Caroline was not alone.
3 Caroline didn't recognize Grand Turk Island.
4 She thought there was no land under her.
5 No one noticed anything.

Mystery 2

Christopher Columbus reported a number of bizarre phenomena in the area as early as October 11 1492. The compass on the ship became unreliable, the sky had a strange light about it and the whole crew noticed on September 15 of that year a huge jet of fire which crossed the sky.

On October 29 1966 a tugboat called The Southern Cities was towing a barge of chemical products in the area. When the tug failed to report in by radio, as it had done every other day, aeroplanes were sent out to see what was wrong. Searchers found the barge intact with all its cargo but, apart from the towing line, the tug and its crew had completely disappeared.

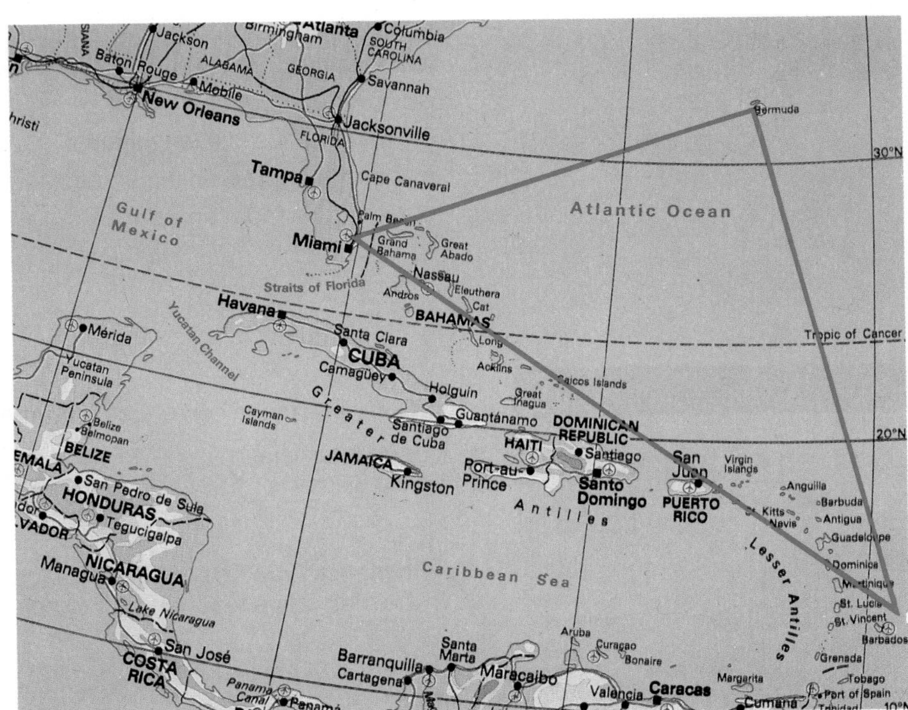

An extract from the coastguards' inquiry report could apply to any one of the boats lost in the area. 'In the absence of distress signals we must conclude that the loss of the tug must have happened so quickly that there was no time to transmit an SOS.'

Match the following words with their definitions.

1 tugboat	☐ pull along
2 compass	☐ international signal for help
3 barge	☐ strange
4 tow	☐ boat that pulls other boats
5 coastguards	☐ instrument for finding directions
6 SOS	☐ undamaged, complete
7 intact	☐ people who keep a check on the sea and shipping
8 bizarre	☐ boat used for carrying heavy loads

Mystery 3

An aeroplane on a routine flight to Miami was being monitored on a radar screen from a control tower as it was coming in to land, when it suddenly disappeared from the screen for a full ten minutes, before reappearing on the screen and then landing normally.

The pilot and the crew of the aeroplane were extremely surprised that the ground crew had been worried and said that nothing unusual had happened. One of the ground crew said to the pilot, 'My friend, for ten minutes you just didn't exist.'

So the pilot and members of the crew looked at their watches and the clock on the aeroplane and discovered that they were ten minutes slower than everyone else's on the control tower. This was even more surprising as twenty minutes before the incident, during a routine pre-landing check, watches on board had been synchronized with watches on the ground.

Put the events in the order they actually happened.

☐ plane disappeared
☐ watches synchronized
☐ plane landed
☐ crew's watches lost ten minutes
☐ plane reappeared on the screen
☐ plane on the radar screen

LEARNING TO LEARN

1 Complete these sentences in as many ways as you can:

1 A good teacher is . . .
2 A good learner is . . .

2 In the end you'll be using language without a teacher. Discuss some of the methods a teacher uses to help you to become 'independent'.

UNIT 12

IF ONLY. . .

Regretting **Wishing and hoping**

A chapter of accidents **Martin Luther King**

A REGRETS

1 Read the article about a honeymoon that went wrong.

1 How many disasters did David and Sandy suffer on their honeymoon?
2 How far is the headline appropriate, do you think?

SANDY TAKES BRIDAL PATH TO MISERY

SANDY ISON will never forget her honeymoon. Not for the romance and kisses but for the disasters.

She and husband David set off in the usual shower of confetti and good wishes and settled into a rented villa at Nice in Southern France.

Troubles began after 22-year-old Sandy from Middleton Cheney, Northamptonshire, became allergic to her wedding ring and had to rip it off her badly swollen finger.

'It's no good being married without a ring on your finger,' she complained. Worse was to come.

They ran out of money for three days because it was a holiday weekend and they were unable to change traveller's cheques. Worse was to come.

Their Porche 911—an £8,000 wedding present to each other—broke down and cost £100 for a clutch cable and tow. Worse was to come. That night the Porsche was stolen.

Sunstroke

The lost car meant that they had to hire another and pay £100 extra insurance. The new car, a BMW, also broke down—clutch again—halfway up an Austrian pass. John, 28, had to negotiate a tortuous 30-mile journey down the mountain in second gear. Worse was to come.

The unhappy couple, who had to spend a night in a hotel at their own expense while the BMW was repaired, had only French money left by now.

With the banks again shut for the weekend they drove for 16 hours 700 miles through Germany back into France where, on the last night of their honeymoon. Sandy went down with a temperature of 104 caused by food poisoning, travel sickness and sunstroke.

'At this point we just wanted to get home', said David yesterday. But their bad luck wasn't over.

Sandy was robbed of £100 at Dover when her purse was stolen. And back home the couple's pet shop was burgled.

'Married life's great if you don't let it get you down,' said Sandy

2 Although Sandy and David don't regret getting married, they have some reservations about their honeymoon. Listen to them talking and note the phrases they use to talk about things they did, things they didn't do and things they blame themselves for.

Things they did	Things they didn't do	Things they blame themselves for

3

Match the phrases on the right with the expressions on the left.

About things they did

1 I wish . . .	have taken our car on honeymoon.
2 Why ever . . .	
3 If only . . .	did we take our car on honeymoon?
4 We shouldn't . . .	
5 Why on earth . . .	we hadn't taken our car on honeymoon.

About things they didn't do

6 We should . . .	have known it was a bank holiday.
7 Why on earth . . .	
8 I wish . . .	we had known it was a bank holiday.
9 If only . . .	
10 Why ever . . .	didn't we know it was a bank holiday?

4

Work in pairs. Imagine you are David, or Sandy, talking to a friend. Tell your partner all your regrets. Your partner could reply like this:

'Don't blame yourself too much.'
'Don't take it so badly.'
'It's just one of those things.'
'You weren't to know, were you?'
'These things happen.'
'I know how you must be feeling.'
'It's not really your fault.'

B

I MUST HAVE BEEN CRAZY . . .

1

Your car broke down on a lonely road when you were driving to London for a busy day of business and social engagements. You decided to take a short cut across the field to the nearest garage, but as you go on you begin to regret not having stayed on the road. What do you think you said to yourself at each stage of your trek? Choose from the alternatives below.

- ☐ I must have been crazy to cross these fields.
- ☐ Perhaps I should have stayed on the road.
- ☐ I simply can't think why I decided this was a short cut!
- ☐ I'm beginning to wish I hadn't come this way.
- ☐ If only I'd stayed on the road!

2

Make suitable expressions of regret for these situations. Your partner replies with appropriate soothing remarks.

1 Last Saturday you went to a party and drank too much – wine and beer. On Sunday you felt so awful you couldn't go out to lunch with your parents as had been arranged. Now they are upset with you.

2 You were offered a partnership in a business for very little investment. Your father thought it was too risky, so you turned it down. Now the business is flourishing and one of the most successful in the area.

3 You bought a new camera a few months ago and lent it to a friend who was going on holiday. Their seven-year-old child played with it and now it's broken.

4 At school you decided to take A-level Italian rather than Biology because you had fallen in love with Mario/Maria while on holiday in Rome the year before. Mario/Maria hasn't written for two years and you've just discovered that the one essential subject for every career that interests you is Biology.

5 Your car had been slow starting for a few days but you hadn't got round to taking it to the garage. Then, last night, in the pouring rain, it wouldn't start at all. You had to leave it outside your friend's house and walk home. You had to get up an hour earlier today because you've got to walk to work – and it's still raining and you've started sneezing!

3

Turn to a new partner and tell him/her about the conversations you've just had, like this:

A:	X regretted	drinking having drunk	so much.

B:	Did he/she? Yes, well, it was	silly! ill-advised! a pity!

4

Have you got any regrets about the past? Think about your educational, business or personal life. Tell a friend!

If I had had better teachers, I	would've might've could've	gone to university. understood maths. passed my exams.

C PRESENT WISHES

1 The hopeful fisherman

Fishing is often a frustrating experience! In frustrating situations we often wish . . .

- (1) things were different (but they aren't)
- (2) someone/something would do something (but they don't)
- (3) we could do something (but we can't)

2

Look at the pictures below and decide what the different people are wishing.

1

2

3

3

If the fishermen in C1 were feeling a bit more optimistic, they might say to themselves:

- I hope it stops raining
- I hope the fish bite
- I hope I catch something

Look back at the pictures in C2 and talk about the people's hopes.

4

What about your wishes and hopes now? Work in small groups or pairs, and write them down. Then compare them with other groups'.

D FUTURE HOPES

1 Listen to this extract from a speech made by Martin Luther King, the American Civil Rights leader, in 1968. He expresses four hopes for the future. What are they? Have any of his dreams come true?

2 What is your vision of the future? How do you hope/expect things will be for you when you are 40/60/80?

E  LEARNING TO LEARN

1 What plans have you got for continuing with your English after this course? Discuss with other students.

2 Have you considered the following strategies? If possible, try and organize some of them before the course finishes.

1 Setting up self-help groups (finding other learners).
2 Finding out how you can receive the BBC World Service.
3 Finding out about, and possibly subscribing to, an English (language) magazine or newspaper.
4 Setting up penfriend networks (possibly with other ex-course members).
5 Continuing English at an evening school.
6 Finding native English-speakers in your home town and making contact.
7 Buying reference books, cassettes, novels etc. before you leave Britain.

REVIEW UNIT 4

PART 1 LANGUAGE REVIEW

Deducing Supposing Speculating Wishing and hoping
Ethnic groups in Britain Carnivals and festivals

A

IT MIGHT BE . . .

Where are these buildings and scenes? Discuss what/where they could be.

B

FESTIVALS

Notting Hill Carnival is 21 years old this year. Pepe Francis, the current administrator of the Carnival Arts Committee, has been involved with the movement for 18 years and, looking back with pride over the achievements of what has now become an important institution in Britain's Black community, says, 'Certainly it's a far cry from 1965 when a single float and a few hundred revellers danced down Golborne Road.'

Last year revellers were estimated at nearly a million and there will be more this year if the weather doesn't play up. On Bank Holiday Sunday and Monday the predominantly grey streets of Notting Hill and Ladbroke Grove will be dramatically transformed by huge colourful living sculptures brought to life by thousands of dancing people. There are a record 76 mas (masquerade) bands taking part this year. There will also be 13 brass bands, 14 steel bands on parade, plus pop, reggae and African groups and concentrated batteries of sound systems.

This year, festivities started remarkably early with top calypsonians like Arrow and David Rudder, giving memorable concerts around London. Caribbean Focus has also brought in many leading Carnival artists and given Caribbean events sustained media coverage as well as the inevitable spin-offs. This influx has generally been good, reflecting an increasingly reciprocal relationship between Black artists here and the Caribbean. 'We took cocoyea mas bands to Mardi Gras in Trinidad and people were quite amazed to see our high-quality costumes,' says Francis.

1 Read the articles. Which group predominantly celebrates the carnival in Notting Hill? What things in particular would appeal to children at the Festival of Chinese Culture in Cardiff?

Festival of Chinese culture

CARDIFF's own Festival of Chinese Culture takes place on Saturday, from 1 to 6 pm, with spectacular displays of martial arts and kite-flying, traditional storytelling, and folk music.

You can sample Dim Sum, Chinese snacks and pastries, learn how to play mahjong or Chinese chess, or have your fortune told according to the age-old art of Yijing.

Children will be able to experiment with face-painting, and turn themselves into characters from Peking Opera and their parents can have traditional water-colours painted for them.

The festival will include lots of demonstrations and takes place at the Chapter Arts Centre, and at the Bute Theatre in the Welsh College of Music and Drama. Entrance is free.

And there's an opportunity on Sunday to hear traditional and modern Chinese music from the internationally renowned Guo brothers of Beijing.

Yi and Yue play many different styles of music, from folk to ancient classical, and their fascinating repertoire includes Peking Opera melodies played on Chinese instruments.

The Guo brothers are in concert at the Sherman Theatre on Sunday at 7.30 pm. Tickets (£4 or £3) are available from the box office.

Cardiff Post, 11/9/86

1 What can you see and do on both occasions?
2 What kind of music can you hear?
3 Which event would you prefer to go to?

2 Unfortunately, that year (1986) it rained very heavily at the Notting Hill Carnival, which disappointed a lot of people. Listen to Beverley telling her friend Anita about her bank holiday. What does she regret about it? What did she most enjoy?

3 Have you been to any similar events which proved disappointing? What did you expect? How were you let down? Exchange stories with a partner.

4 With a new partner, either report your discussions in B3 or, using the dialogue in B2, imagine you are Anita telling another friend how Beverley enjoyed the day.

C

HINDU HOPES

1 The Hindu Community in London are hoping to build the new temple shown in picture 4 on page 86. Read this article about it.

HINDUS hoping to build a magnificent £5 million temple complex in Kenton have released the first drawings of the building.

A public inquiry into the temple plans, backed by Brent but opposed by neighbouring Harrow Council, closed on August 15.

The 60 ft temple at the centre of the complex would be modelled on the Taj Mahal, with detailed hand crafted carvings, arches, domes and spires built of imported Indian white marble and tipped with gold.

The 21,000 strong Swaminarayan Mission in Britain has applied to build the religious centre on the site of the Old Harrow School playing fields, adjoining the grounds of Northwick Park Hospital.

Now listen to two local residents who seem to have got hold of the wrong end of the stick. How many 'facts' do they get wrong? What are they?

2 Having a building constructed as you want it to be isn't always easy. The problem is provoking a lot of discussion among the Hindu Community itself. How do you think they feel? Discuss their reactions, using the words below.

hope

expect

wonder if

am dying for

am longing for

can't wait for

D

WORDS OF COMFORT

1 Although many of the multicultural communities are well established in Britain, there are always new arrivals. What are the particular problems of the Asian women in the following article?

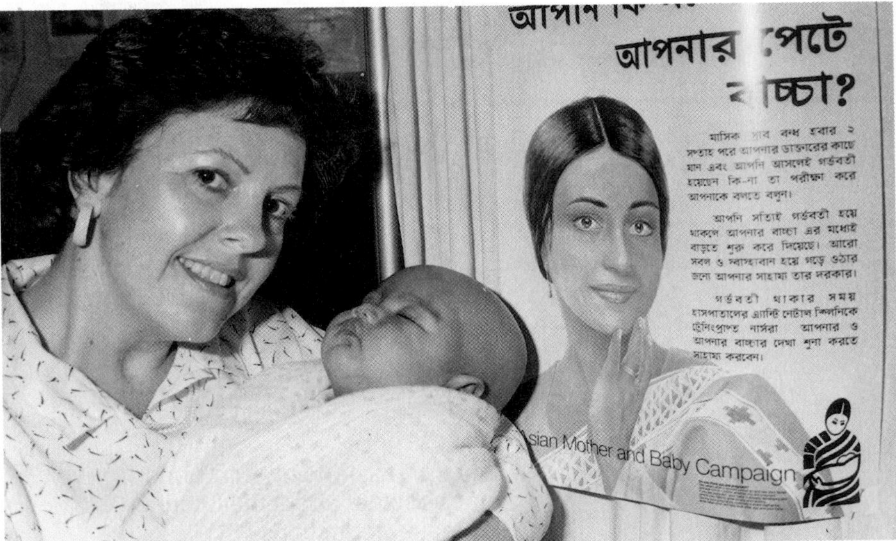

PREGNANT Asian women in Cardiff who cannot speak English can now have language lessons in their homes.

Riverside Community Centre has trained more home tutors to teach ''English for Pregnancy''.

So far, 20 tutors have been helping pregnant Asian women – in fact, most of their ''students'' have now had their babies.

Scared

One of the ''students'', in Grangetown, who is now a proud mum, said: ''I couldn't have managed without my home tutor's help. It was my first baby, my husband was away, I have no relatives nearby and I was so scared''.

Support

One home tutor, Mrs Ceri James, of Llandaff, said: ''Obviously I was a little apprehensive at first. But I saw the advert for tutors and realized I'd had so much support when I was pregnant, from my husband, family and friends.

''I couldn't help wondering how confusing it must be for a woman giving birth in a strange country where they speak a strange language and when she's going through a time of emotional stress.''

2 Place yourself in the position of these Asian women and discuss . . .

1 how the situation would be easier for you (e.g. 'If I spoke better English, I wouldn't need a tutor').
2 your hopes for your children.

3 The Swan Report (1984) affirmed that multicultural education should be an integral part of the British school curriculum. In what ways do you think this could be implemented, and what effect could it have on the next generation. Speculate!

PART 2 COURSE REVIEW

Ways out and on

A ASSESSMENT

1 Below is a list of the language items you have studied in Units 10–12; the numbers in brackets refer to the units. Grade yourself according to how well you think you can now do these things.

√√√ very well
√√ quite well
√ need more practice

Can you . . .

express certainty and uncertainty (10)?
speculate about the future (10)?
make deductions (11)?
express regrets (12)?
express wishes and hopes (12)?
be imaginative in English (12)?
organize your own learning (12)?

2 You have now reached the end of *Fast Forward 2*. We hope you have made progress. Take a few minutes to think about some of the things you have learned.

1 Write a few sentences about the things you liked or feel you have learned well.

I liked the exercise on . . . . . because . . . . .
I enjoyed . . . . .
I found . . . . . very useful . . . . .

2 Write down the things you still need to do a lot of work on.

3 Write down five things you are going to do when you get home to help you improve your English.

Compare your list with your neighbour's.

3 Use the following questions to start a group discussion.

How do you feel about . . .

your progress in English?
the experience of being a student again?
Britain and its people and culture?

What were the best things about the whole course experience for you?

B

LANGUAGE REVIEW

Match the questions in A with the appropriate answers in B.

A

1 What do you think of boxing?
2 I'd like to present Mrs McKenzie.
3 Excuse me, can you tell me the way to George Street?
4 What do you suggest I do?
5 What can I get you?
6 Could you open the window?
7 How about going to the cinema tonight?
8 Why on earth did we buy this car? It's not very good.
9 I'm sorry but I bought this shirt yesterday and it's got no buttons.
10 Which country has the highest GNP per head?
11 How would you feel if you were going to China for 6 months?
12 What'll you do if you fail your exams?
13 There's someone at the door.

B

☐ A scotch and soda please.
☐ I'd feel very excited.
☐ I'm sorry, sir, would you like to exchange it?
☐ Sorry, I'm a stranger here myself.
☐ What a good idea!
☐ I expect I'll take them again.
☐ The USA does.
☐ How do you do?
☐ Don't know really.
☐ It must be Fred.
☐ You weren't to know, were you?
☐ Why don't you sleep on it?
☐ Yes, of course.

C

LAST LINES

In pairs or small groups, choose one of the following 'last lines' and make up a dialogue which led up to it. Act the scene to another group.

1 Well, I hope it doesn't happen again!
2 No thanks, we're just looking.
3 Well, I suppose I could, but I'll need it back on Friday.
4 I know what you mean – it's a corkscrew!
5 Well, I think we'll have to agree to differ there.
6 Well, I don't mind, really.
7 Well, it must have been him then.
8 I'm afraid I do mind actually.
9 Oh, I'd love that, but it's only a dream.
10 It's just one of those things.

D

THE LEAVING OF LIVERPOOL

1 Write down six words that you immediately think of when you hear the word 'leaving'. Compare your words with those of other students.

2 Listen to the song and find the following names:

- a river in the north-west of England
- where the singer is going
- which town he is leaving
- the name of his ship
- the name of his captain

3 Listen to the chorus again and fill in the missing words.

. . . . . . fare thee well, my . . . . . . true . . . . . .
When I . . . . we . . . . . . be
It's . . . . . . the . . . . of Liverpool . . . . . . grieves . . . . . .
But my . . . . when I . . . . thee.

In line three, does 'grieves me' mean . . . .

- gets on my nerves?
- worries me?
- causes me deep suffering?

4 The words 'fare' and 'bound' each have more than one meaning in English. In the song they appear in the phrases below. Put a circle around the correct meaning of each phrase.

. . . fare thee well . . .

- pay a lot of money
- a display of food
- make progress
- say goodbye

. . . bound for . . .

- limited by
- jump on
- going to
- certain to

5 Listen to Verses 1 and 2 of the song again and put the following lines in the correct order.

☐ *But you know I'll write to you a letter*
☐ *A place that I know right well*
☐ *For I'm bound for California*
☐ *Yes I'm bound for California*
☐ *Me love, when I'm homeward bound*
☐ *Fare thee well the Prince's Landing Stage*
☐ *By way of the stormy Cape Horn*
☐ *River Mersey, fare thee well*

6 How does the singer feel about leaving Liverpool? Would any of the words that you thought of in exercise 1 be true for him? Discuss your ideas with the other students.